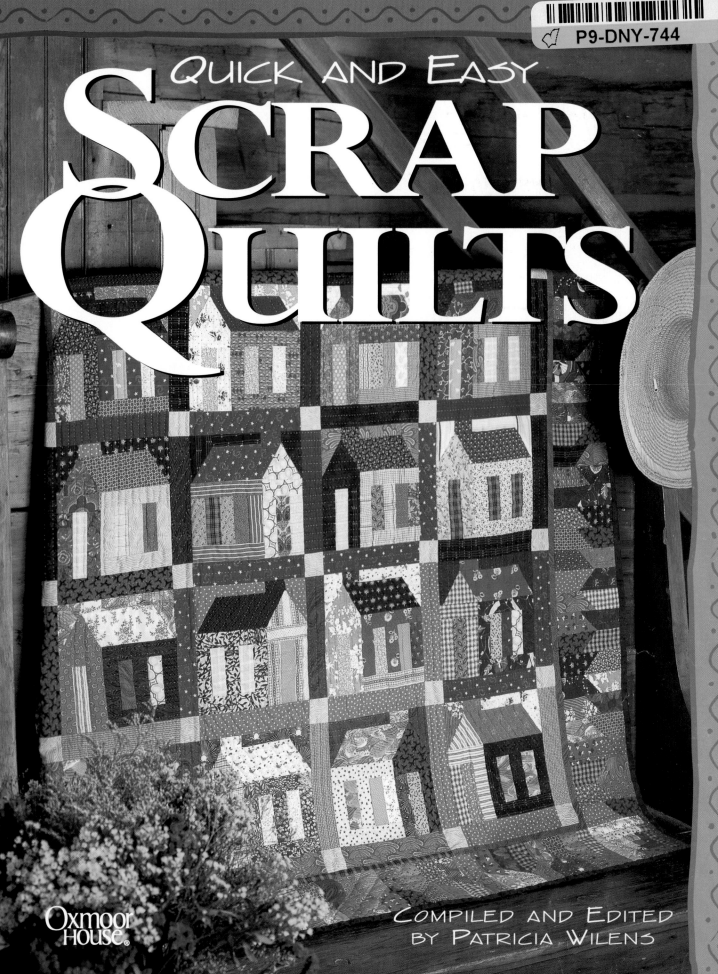

Quick and Easy
SCRAP QUILTS

Oxmoor House®

COMPILED AND EDITED
BY PATRICIA WILENS

Quick and Easy Scrap Quilts
From the *For the Love of Quilting* series
©1995 by Oxmoor House, Inc.
Book Division of Southern Progress Corporation
P.O. Box 2463, Birmingham, Alabama 35201

Published by Oxmoor House, Inc., and
Leisure Arts, Inc.

Library of Congress Catalog Card
   Number: 95-69096
Hardcover ISBN: 0-8487-1448-2
Softcover ISBN: 0-8487-1462-8
Manufactured in the United States of America
Eighth Printing 1998

Editor-in-Chief: Nancy Fitzpatrick Wyatt
Senior Crafts Editor: Susan Ramey Cleveland
Senior Editor, Editorial Services: Olivia K. Wells
Art Director: James Boone

Quick and Easy Scrap Quilts
Editor: Patricia Wilens
Copy Editor: Susan S. Cheatham
Editorial Assistant: Wendy L. Wolford
Designer/Illustrator: Emily Albright Parrish
Technical Illustrator: Carol Loria
Senior Photographer: John O'Hagan
Photo Stylist: Katie Stoddard
Production and Distribution Director: Phillip Lee
Production Manager: Gail Morris
Associate Production Manager: Theresa L. Beste
Production Assistants: Valerie Heard,
   Marianne Jordan Wilson

Where to write to us: For billing, shipping, and
other business inquiries, write to Oxmoor House
Customer Relations, 500 Office Park Drive,
Birmingham, AL 35223. If you have a question or
comment regarding the content of this book, please
write to Scrap Quilts Editor, P.O. Box 2262,
Birmingham, AL 35201.

INTRO

All quilts are acts of love, but scrap quilts even more so. They embody love of color, love of creativity, and love of things practical and useful. Most of all, scrap quilts confirm how much we love fabric. The colorful prints, the textures, oh, the glorious variety of fabric! I owe a debt of gratitude to two women who taught me to love fabric.

In the basement of our house, my grandmother kept a cedar chest filled with remnants of a millinery career. I spent many a childhood hour rummaging through that chest, playing with velvet and lace. A yard of bright satin, draped toga-style, was my make-believe Cinderella gown to wear to Prince Charming's ball.

My youth is colored with memories of wonderful dresses that Mamaw made with unerring artistry. The cedar chest yielded a yellow satin from which she made my first formal, as well as scraps of fabric and lace for prom dresses and wedding veils, all crafted with love.

DUCTION

Most of what I know about quiltmaking is a gift from Marti Michell, a pioneer in the quilting "revival" who gave me my first job in this field. We all aspire to first-class workmanship, but Marti has fun, too. With typical good humor, she doesn't feel guilty about having lots of fabric. To Marti, a fabric collection improves with age and a scrap is "any piece of fabric I haven't used yet."

Today's quilts can be made with tools and techniques that my grandmother would envy. Rotary cutting and quick piecing make patchwork faster and easier than ever. In this book, instructions are written to reap the benefits of these time-savers. If you're not familiar with these ways and means, review the *Start to Finish* section—this introduction to basic quiltmaking will get you started. Sprinkled throughout the book, you'll find more helpful hints called *Pin Points*.

My grandmother's sewing days are gone and I see Marti rarely now. But they inspired me to collect stacks of cotton fabric and I'm stingy about parting with any of it, even old calicoes that I don't really like any more. I want to find a project for every piece, like the wonderful quilts in this book. I also have bits of braid and trim, which I vow to use someday, that retain a faint fragrance of cedar.

The lessons I learned are like scraps of faith. The love of fabric is a hope that one day a little piece will make a memory.

Patricia Wilens

THE SCRAP QUILT COLLECTION

CONTENTS

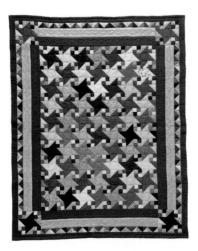

PIN POINTS

START TO FINISH: BASIC QUILTMAKING TECHNIQUES

FABRIC FROLIC

Select one dark, neutral fabric—black, brown, or navy—for this quilt's sashing and borders, and then anything goes! These blocks are a freewheeling mix of many prints. The neutral fabric holds it all together.

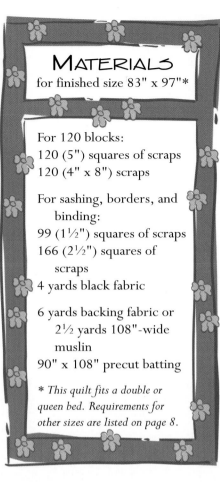

For 120 blocks:
120 (5") squares of scraps
120 (4" x 8") scraps

For sashing, borders, and
   binding:
99 (1½") squares of scraps
166 (2½") squares of
   scraps
4 yards black fabric

6 yards backing fabric or
   2½ yards 108"-wide
   muslin
90" x 108" precut batting

*This quilt fits a double or
queen bed. Requirements for
other sizes are listed on page 8.*

CUTTING

Cut all strips cross-grain unless stated
otherwise.

From 4" x 8" scraps, cut:
• 2 (4") squares. Then cut each square in
   half diagonally to get a total of 4 triangles from each fabric.

From black fabric, cut:
• 1 (32") square for bias binding or 9
   (2½"-wide) strips for straight-grain
   binding.
• 2 (3" x 97") lengthwise strips and 2
   (3" x 87") lengthwise strips for outer
   border.
• 2 (1½" x 90") lengthwise strips and 2
   (1½" x 78") lengthwise strips for
   inner border.
• 218 (1½" x 6¾") sashing strips.

MAKING BLOCKS

Finished size of block is 6¼" square.
1. Pair 1 set of 4 triangles with 1 (5")
square.
2. Fold square in half vertically and
horizontally, finger-pressing a crease in
each direction.
3. With right sides facing, match long
raw edge of 1 triangle to 1 side of square
(Diagram A). Align triangle's point with
crease. (Triangle is slightly longer than
square, so triangle extends a bit at corners.) Stitch seam. Repeat to sew triangle to opposite side of square.
4. Press both triangles to right side.
5. Sew 2 more triangles to remaining
sides of square (Diagram B). Press to right
sides to complete block (Diagram C).
6. Make 120 blocks. Square up blocks
to 6¾" x 6¾".

JOINING BLOCKS

This quilt is an example of a straight set
with sashing, with the blocks set 10 x 12.
See setting illustration on page 149.
1. Lay out blocks in 12 horizontal
rows, with 10 blocks in each row (Row
Assembly Diagram). Position 9 sashing
strips between blocks as shown. When
satisfied with placement, join blocks and
sashing in each row. Press seam allowances toward sashing.
2. Lay out remaining sashing strips in
11 horizontal rows, with 10 strips in
each row and 9 (1½") squares between
strips (Row Assembly Diagram). Join
strips and squares in each row. Press
seam allowances toward sashing.
3. Lay out all rows, alternating block
rows and sashing rows as shown in
photo. Join rows. Press seam allowances
toward sashing. (Continued)

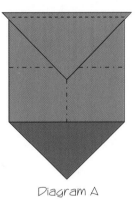

Diagram A

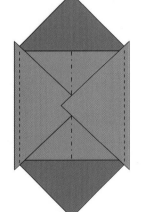

Diagram B

Diagram C

Row Assembly

ADDING BORDERS

1. Referring to instructions on page 150, measure quilt from top to bottom; then trim 1½" x 90" black inner borders to match length. Join borders to quilt sides. Press seam allowances toward borders.

2. Measure quilt from side to side; then trim 1½" x 78" black inner border to match quilt width. Join border to quilt top. Repeat for bottom border. Press seam allowances toward borders.

3. For pieced border, join 44 (2½") squares in a row for each side border and 39 squares each for top and bottom borders. Join side borders to quilt. Press seam allowances toward black inner border. Join top and bottom borders to quilt in same manner. (*Note:* If pieced border doesn't fit precisely, add more squares or subtract a few as necessary.)

4. Measure quilt as before; then trim 3"-wide black strips as needed to make outer side borders. Join borders to quilt sides. Press seam allowances toward borders. Add borders to top and bottom edges in same manner.

FINISHING

1. Divide backing fabric into 2 (3-yard) lengths. Cut 1 piece in half lengthwise. Sew a narrow panel to each side of wide panel. Press seam allowances toward narrow panels.

2. On quilt shown, an X is quilted in each block, plus a line through the horizontal center. Two other quilting suggestions are shown here (Alternate Quilting Diagrams). Mark desired quilting designs on quilt top.

3. Layer backing, batting, and quilt top. Baste. Quilt as desired.

4. Make 10 yards of bias or straight-grain binding. See pages 158 and 159 for instructions on making and applying binding.

VARIABLE SIZES

Size	Wall/Crib	Twin	King
Finished Size	39" x 53½"	68" x 90"	99" x 107"
Number of Blocks	24	88	156
Blocks Set	4 x 6	8 x 11	12 x 13
Number of Sashing Strips	38	157	287
Border Width (Finished size)	1", 2", 2½"	1", 2", 2½"	1", 2", 2½"

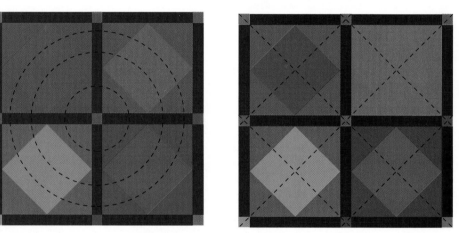

Alternate Quilting Diagrams

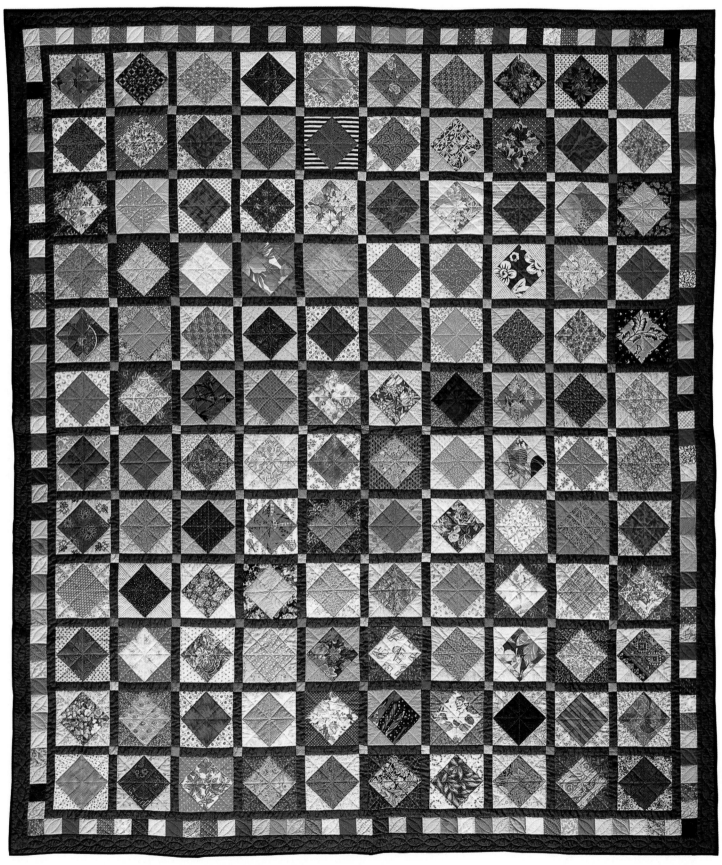

Quilt by Eleanor Hagen Maloney of Atlantic Beach, Florida

A Change of Heart

The ever popular heart introduces many a stitcher to appliqué because it has the curves and points needed for practice. This little wall hanging will help you learn to love appliqué.

MATERIALS
for finished size 20" x 20"

For 53 blocks:
53 (2") squares of scraps
53 (3") squares of scraps

For sashing and binding:
⅝ yard purple fabric
24" square backing fabric
24" square batting

This quilt is a wall hanging. Requirements for other sizes are listed on page 13.

CUTTING

Before cutting, choose an appliqué technique. Directions on cutting pieces for hand appliqué are on page 144. Make template from small heart pattern at right. Add seam allowance when cutting fabric.

Cut all strips cross-grain.

From 2" squares, cut:
• 53 hearts.

From purple fabric, cut:
• 15" square for continuous bias binding or 3 (2"-wide) strips for straight-grain binding.
• 4 (1¾" x 20") sashing strips.

MAKING BLOCKS

Finished size of block is 2½" square.
1. Prepare hearts for appliqué. Directions on preparing pieces for hand appliqué are on page 147.
2. Fold each square in half, finger-pressing a center crease for a placement guide.
3. For each block, select 1 heart and 1 square. Pair fabrics to obtain good contrast in each block.
4. Center heart on each square, aligning center points of heart with placement guide. Pin or baste heart in place.
5. Appliqué hearts to complete 53 blocks.

JOINING BLOCKS

1. Lay out 25 blocks in 5 horizontal rows, with 5 blocks in each row (Row Assembly Diagram). If desired, arrange blocks by value as shown in photo, with lightest squares in upper left corner and darkest squares at bottom right. When satisfied with placement, join blocks in each row. Press seam allowances in opposite directions from row to row.
2. Join rows to complete center section.

(Continued)

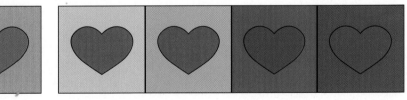

Row Assembly Diagram

Pattern for Other Sizes

Pattern for Wall Hanging

ADDING SASHING

1. Referring to instructions on page 150, measure length of wall hanging; then trim 2 sashing strips to match length. Join 1 strip to each side of wall hanging. Press seam allowances toward sashing.

2. Measure width of wall hanging; then trim 2 sashing strips to match width. Join 1 strip each to top and bottom of wall hanging.

ADDING BORDER

1. Lay out blocks around quilt top to form border (see photo). When satisfied with placement, join 6 blocks in a vertical row for each side border. Join borders to quilt sides.

2. Join 8 blocks in a horizontal row and join to top of quilt. Repeat for bottom border.

FINISHING

1. On quilt shown, hearts are outline-quilted and 2 parallel lines are quilted in sashing. Mark desired quilting designs on quilt top.

2. Layer backing, batting, and quilt top. Baste. Quilt as desired.

3. Make 2¾ yards of bias or straight-grain binding. See pages 158 and 159 for instructions on making and applying binding.

4. See page 23 for tips on making a hanging sleeve.

Quilt by Nancy Wagner Graves of Manhattan, Kansas

VARIABLE SIZES

Size	Twin	Double/Queen	King
Finished Size	50" x 80"	75" x 90"	80" x 90"
Finished Size of Block	5"	5"	5"
Number of Blocks	139	216	259
Inner Blocks Set	7 x 13	11 x 14	13 x 15
Border Blocks Set	10 x 16	15 x 18	16 x 18
Sashing Width (finished size)	2½"	2½"	2½"

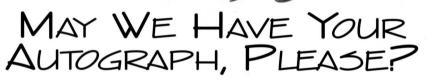

Pin Points

MAY WE HAVE YOUR AUTOGRAPH, PLEASE?

It's important to sign and date your quilt, because it is the legacy of tomorrow. Most antique quilts offer few clues about their origin, leaving empty pages where there should be history about women and family. We owe it to future generations to leave a record of our quilts and who made them.

There are several ways to permanently mark a quilt, on either the front or back. Incorporating your name and a date in the quilting is a time-honored method, as is embroidering these details on the quilt top or backing.

Many quilters like to sew a signature patch onto the backing. In addition to a signature, this label might include your home town, the date that the quilt was completed, who it was made for and why, and any group or occasion connected with the quilt. You might also inscribe instructions for washing the quilt, for the benefit of future generations.

The most practical label is a piece of muslin, hemmed on all sides. Press plastic-coated freezer paper to the back to stabilize the fabric for writing. Use a fine-tip permanent pen to write your message. Peel off the paper; then handstitch the label to the quilt back.

A change of heart?

Nancy Wagner Graves
Manhattan, Kansas
1993

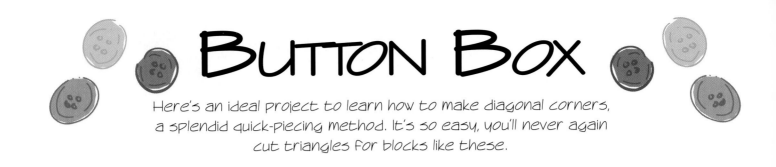

BUTTON BOX

Here's an ideal project to learn how to make diagonal corners,
a splendid quick-piecing method. It's so easy, you'll never again
cut triangles for blocks like these.

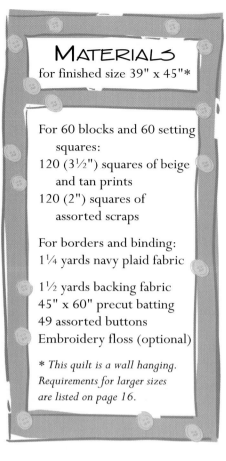

MATERIALS
for finished size 39" x 45"*

For 60 blocks and 60 setting squares:
120 (3½") squares of beige and tan prints
120 (2") squares of assorted scraps

For borders and binding:
1¼ yards navy plaid fabric

1½ yards backing fabric
45" x 60" precut batting
49 assorted buttons
Embroidery floss (optional)

*This quilt is a wall hanging. Requirements for larger sizes are listed on page 16.

CUTTING
Cut all strips cross-grain.

From navy plaid, cut:
- 4 (5"-wide) strips for border.
- 1 (24") square for bias binding or 4 (2½"-wide) strips for straight-grain binding.

MAKING BLOCKS
Finished size of block is 3" square.

1. Select 60 (3½") squares for diagonal corners. Set remainder aside.

2. See page 17 for tips on how to make diagonal corners. Using assorted 2" squares, make diagonal corners on 2 opposite corners of each 3½" square (Block Diagram).

3. Make 60 blocks with diagonal corners. Square up blocks to 3½" x 3½".

Block Diagram

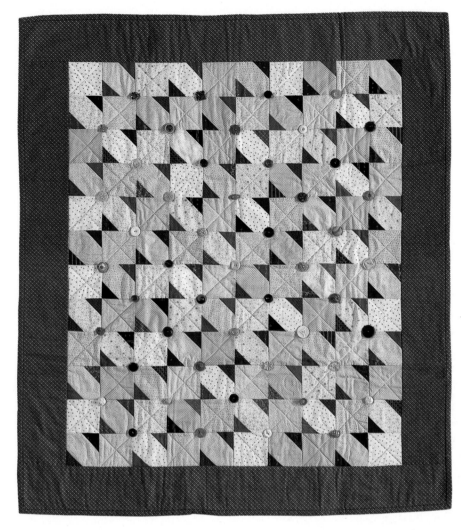

Quilt by Sharon K. Morton of North Olmsted, Ohio

JOINING BLOCKS

This quilt is an example of a straight set with alternating pieced and plain blocks. The blocks are set 10 x 12. See setting illustration on page 149.

1. Lay out 12 horizontal rows of 10 blocks each, alternating 5 plain squares and 5 pieced blocks (Row Assembly Diagram). Lay out 6 of Row 1, starting with a plain square, and 6 of Row 2, starting with a pieced block. When satisfied with placement, join blocks in each row. Press seam allowances toward plain squares.

2. Join rows, alternating rows 1 and 2 as shown in photo. (Continued)

Row 1—Make 6.

Row 2—Make 6.

Row Assembly Diagram

ADDING BORDERS

1. Referring to instructions on page 150, measure quilt; then trim 2 navy plaid borders to match length. Join borders to quilt sides. Press seam allowances toward borders.

2. Measure quilt width and trim 2 borders to match. Join borders to quilt top and bottom. Press seam allowances toward borders.

FINISHING

1. On quilt shown, an X is machine-quilted in each plain square. Two alternative quilting designs are shown here (*Alternate Quilting Diagrams*). **Mark desired quilting designs on quilt top.**

2. Layer backing, batting, and quilt top. Baste. Quilt as desired.

3. Referring to photo, position a button where 4 unpieced corners meet. Sew buttons in place or tie with embroidery floss as desired. *Note:* Don't use buttons on quilts intended for a home with small children.

4. Make 4¾ yards of bias or straight-grain binding. See pages 158 and 159 for instructions on making and applying binding.

5. See page 23 for tips on making a hanging sleeve.

VARIABLE SIZES

Size	Twin	Double/Queen	King
Finished Size	64" x 74"	86" x 98"	98" x 98"
Finished Size of Block	5"	6"	6"
Number of Plain Squares	60	84	98
Number of Pieced Blocks	60	84	98
Cutting	120 (5½") sqs 120 (3") sqs	168 (6½") sqs 168 (3½") sqs	196 (6½") sqs 196 (3½") sqs
Blocks Set	10 x 12	12 x 14	14 x 14
Border Width (finished size)	7"	7"	7"

Alternate Quilting Diagrams

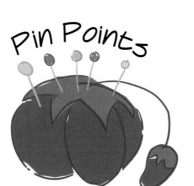

Pin Points

Sew Quick Diagonal Corners

This quick-piecing technique turns squares into sewn triangles with a stitch and a snip. By sewing squares to squares, you don't have to juggle seam allowances, which can be difficult with triangles. This method requires a bit more fabric, but the ease and speed with which you'll sew these corners is well worth a little waste.

Project instructions state size of both fabric pieces needed. The base fabric is either a square or a rectangle, but the contrasting corner always starts out as a square.

Before sewing, you need to make a seam guide that will enable you to machine-stitch diagonal lines without marking the fabric beforehand. Draw a 5"-long line on graph paper. Place the paper on the sewing machine and bring the needle down through the line. Use a ruler to verify that the line is straight and parallel to the needle. Tape the paper in place. Trim the top edge of the paper as needed to leave the needle and presser foot unobstructed.

1. With right sides facing, match the small square to one corner of the base square. Align the top tip of the small square with the needle and the bottom tip with the seam guide. Stitch from corner to corner through both layers, keeping the bottom tip of the small square in line with the seam guide to sew a straight seam.

2. Press the small square in half at the seam.

3. Trim the fabric from the back of the stitched corner, leaving a ¼" seam allowance.

You can repeat the procedure to add a diagonal corner to two, three, or all four corners of the base square.

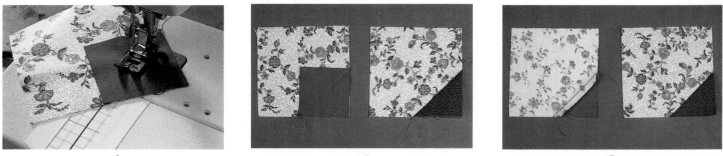

1   2   3

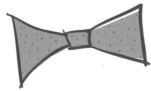 # BOW TIES

Pink and green scraps form diagonal lines of big and little bow ties across this quilt. Have fun experimenting with different sets and color variations; how about bright prints on a black background? The easy diagonal-corner technique makes fast work of this updated traditional block.

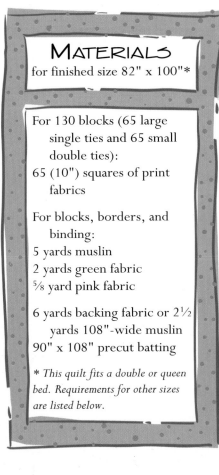

MATERIALS
for finished size 82" x 100"*

For 130 blocks (65 large single ties and 65 small double ties):
65 (10") squares of print fabrics

For blocks, borders, and binding:
5 yards muslin
2 yards green fabric
⅝ yard pink fabric

6 yards backing fabric or 2½ yards 108"-wide muslin
90" x 108" precut batting

This quilt fits a double or queen bed. Requirements for other sizes are listed below.

CUTTING

Cut all strips cross-grain unless stated otherwise.

From *each* print fabric, cut:
• 2 (3½") squares.
• 6 (2") squares.
• 4 (1¼") squares.

From muslin, cut:
• 2 (3½" x 72") and 2 (3½" x 84") lengthwise strips for first border.
• 2 (3½" x 82") and 2 (3½" x 94") lengthwise strips for third border.
• 260 (3½") squares.
• 260 (2") squares.

From pink fabric, cut:
• 8 (2½"-wide) strips for second border.

From green fabric, cut:
• 1 (32") square for bias binding or 9 (2½"-wide) strips for straight-grain binding.
• 9 (3½"-wide) strips for fourth border.

MAKING BLOCKS

Finished size of block is 6" square. Sixty-five blocks are single large bow ties and 65 blocks are four-patches of small ties and solid squares. Make large ties first.

1. See page 17 for tips on making diagonal corners. Using 2" squares of scrap fabric, stitch 1 corner on each of 130 (3½") muslin squares.

2. For each block, select 2 (3½") squares of 1 scrap fabric and 2 muslin squares with corners of that same scrap fabric. Arrange units in 2 horizontal rows (Block 1 Assembly Diagram). Join units in each row; then join rows to complete block.

3. Make 65 large tie blocks. Square up blocks to 6½" x 6½".

4. For small ties, use 1¼" squares of scrap fabric to make diagonal corners on 130 (2") squares of muslin. Join these with 2" squares of matching scrap fabric as before (Block 1 Assembly Diagram) to make 130 small ties.

5. For each four-patch block, select 2 small ties and 2 (3½") squares of muslin. Arrange units in 2 horizontal rows (Block 2 Assembly Diagram). Join units in each row; then join rows to complete block.

6. Make 65 four-patch tie blocks. Square up blocks to 6½" x 6½".

(Continued)

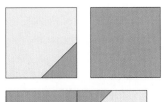

Block 1 Assembly Diagram

Block 2 Assembly Diagram

VARIABLE SIZES

Size	Wall/Crib	Twin	King
Finished Size	52" x 52"	70" x 94"	94" x 106"
Number of Large Bow Tie Blocks	24	48	84
Number of Four-Patch Bow Tie Blocks	25	48	84
Blocks Set	7 x 7	8 x 12	12 x 14
Border Widths (Finished size)	2", 3"	3", 2", 3", 3"	3", 2", 3", 3"

JOINING BLOCKS

This quilt is an example of a straight set with alternating blocks. The blocks are set 10 x 13. See setting illustration on page 149.

1. Lay out 13 horizontal rows of 10 blocks each, alternating large tie blocks and four-patches (Row Assembly Diagram). Lay out 7 of Row 1, starting with a four-patch, and 6 of Row 2, starting with a large tie block. When satisfied with placement, join blocks in each row. Press seam allowances toward large tie blocks.

2. Join rows, alternating rows as shown in photo.

ADDING BORDERS

1. Referring to instructions on page 150, measure quilt; then trim 2 (84") muslin borders to match length. Join borders to quilt sides. Press seam allowances toward borders.

2. Measure quilt width and trim 2 (72") muslin borders to match. Join borders to quilt top and bottom.

3. For second border, join 2 pink border strips end-to-end for each border. Repeat steps 1 and 2 to join borders to quilt top.

4. For third border, measure and trim remaining muslin borders to fit. Join muslin borders to quilt top in same manner.

5. For fourth border, measure quilt as before and piece green border strips to fit. Join borders to quilt sides; then join borders to top and bottom.

FINISHING

1. Divide backing fabric into 2 (3-yard) lengths. Cut 1 piece in half lengthwise. Sew a narrow panel to each side of wide panel. Press seam allowances toward narrow panels.

2. On quilt shown, bow ties are outline-quilted. Two alternative quilting designs are shown here (Alternate Quilting Diagrams). Mark desired quilting designs on quilt top.

3. Layer backing, batting, and quilt top. Baste. Quilt as desired.

4. Make 10¼ yards of bias or straight-grain binding. See pages 158 and 159 for instructions on making and applying binding.

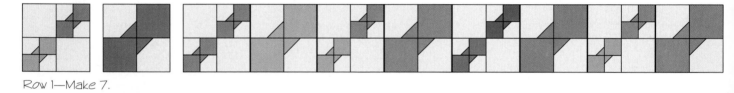

Row 1—Make 7.

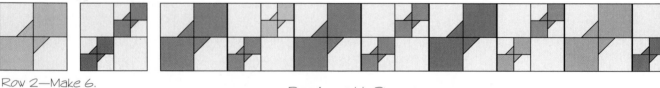

Row 2—Make 6.

Row Assembly Diagram

Alternate Quilting Diagrams

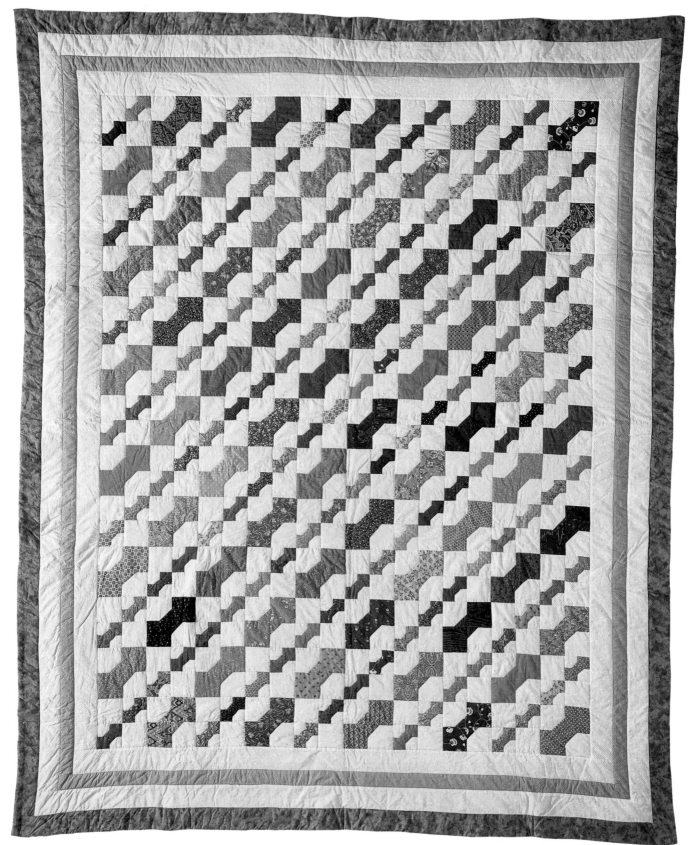

Quilt by Helen Johnstone of Glendora, New Jersey

KALEIDOSCOPE

The illusion of circular halos in this quilt is created by the interplay
of light and dark fabrics. You won't see these rings of light
in individual blocks, but they appear when blocks are joined.

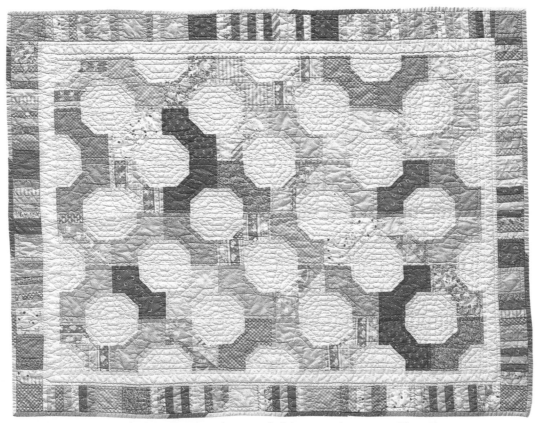

Quilt by Diana Hines of Winter Springs, Florida

Pin Points

HANGING AROUND

Hanging a quilt on the wall adds color and drama to any decor. However, it is important to protect a quilt while showing it off. Only a sturdy, lightweight quilt should be hung. If a quilt is in delicate condition, hanging will only hasten its deterioration.

Do not use pushpins or tacks to hang a quilt because the metal can leave rust stains on the fabric.

The method most often used to hang a quilt is to sew a sleeve on the back so a dowel can be slipped through it. This method distributes the weight evenly across the width of the quilt.

1. From leftover backing fabric, cut an 8"-wide piece that is the same length as the quilt edge. On each end, turn under ½";

then turn under another ½". Topstitch to hem both ends. With wrong sides facing, fold the fabric in half lengthwise and stitch the long edges together. Press seam allowances open and to the middle of the sleeve.

2. Center the sleeve on the quilt backing about 1" below the binding with the seam against the backing. Hand-sew the sleeve to the quilt through backing and batting along both long edges. For large quilts, make two or three sleeve sections as shown so you can use more nails or brackets to support the dowel to better distribute the quilt's weight.

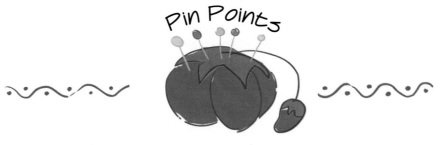

1

2

KALEIDOSCOPE

The illusion of circular halos in this quilt is created by the interplay of light and dark fabrics. You won't see these rings of light in individual blocks, but they appear when blocks are joined.

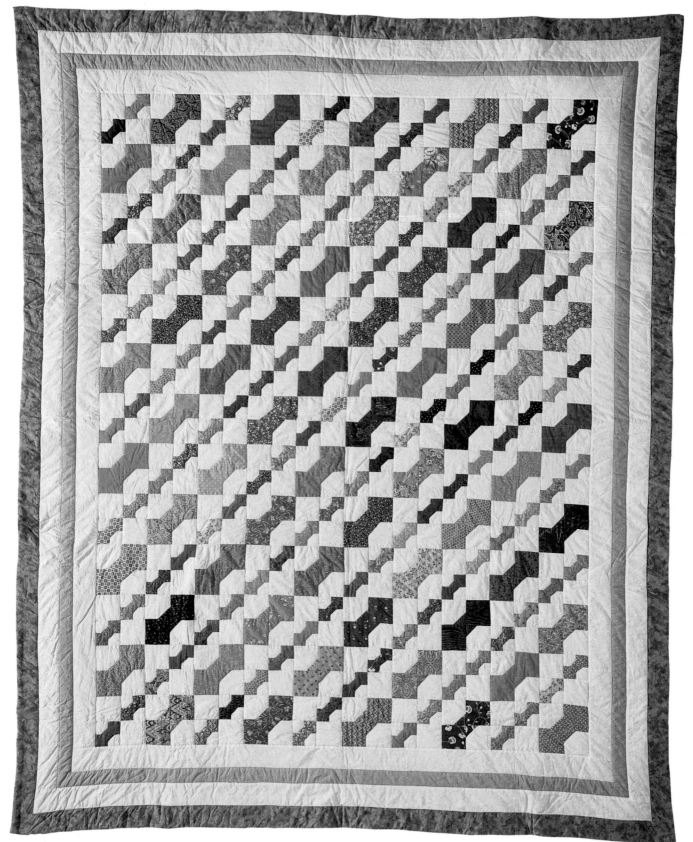

Quilt by Helen Johnstone of Glendora, New Jersey

BABY BOWS

Use the quick diagonal-corner technique to make little blocks for this baby version of the grown-up Bow Ties Quilt.

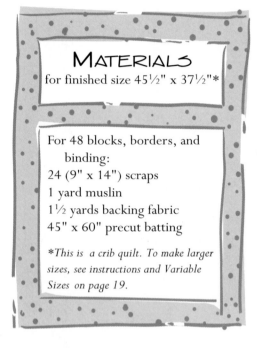

MATERIALS
for finished size 45½" x 37½"*

For 48 blocks, borders, and
    binding:
24 (9" x 14") scraps
1 yard muslin
1½ yards backing fabric
45" x 60" precut batting

*This is a crib quilt. To make larger sizes, see instructions and Variable Sizes on page 19.

CUTTING
Cut all strips cross-grain.

From *each* scrap fabric, cut:
• 5 (3") squares.
• 4 (1¾") squares.
• 6 (1¼" x 3") strips for outer border.

From muslin, cut:
• 4 (1¾"-wide) strips for inner border.
• 96 (3") squares.

MAKING BLOCKS
Finished size of block is 5" square.
1. See page 17 for tips on making diagonal corners. Using 1¾" squares, stitch 1 corner on each muslin square.
2. Referring to block assembly instructions on page 19, join 2 (3") print squares and 2 (3") muslin squares for each block.
3. Make 48 blocks. Square up blocks to 5½" x 5½".

JOINING BLOCKS
This quilt is a straight set with block units set 4 x 3. See setting illustration on page 149.
1. Join blocks in groups of 4 (Unit Diagram).
2. Lay out 3 horizontal rows with 4 four-block units in each row (Row Assembly Diagram). Join units in each row; then join rows.

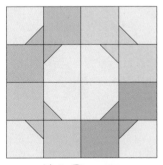

Unit Diagram

ADDING BORDERS
1. Referring to instructions on page 150, measure quilt; then trim 2 muslin borders to match length. Join borders to quilt sides. Press seam allowances toward borders.
2. Measure quilt width and trim 2 borders to match. Join borders to quilt top and bottom.
3. Join 5 (3") print squares and 40 (1¼" x 3") assorted strips for each long border. Comparing border to side of quilt, add or subtract small strips as needed for length. Join borders to long sides of quilt.
4. Join 7 squares and 27 strips for short border, with a square at each end. Add or subtract strips as needed to fit. Sew border to short edge. Repeat for opposite border.

FINISHING
1. On quilt shown, echo quilting on muslin emphasizes bow ties. Mark desired quilting designs on quilt top.
2. Layer backing, batting, and quilt top. Baste. Quilt as desired.
3. Cut 2"-wide strips from remaining print scraps for binding. See pages 158 and 159 for instructions on joining strips and applying binding.

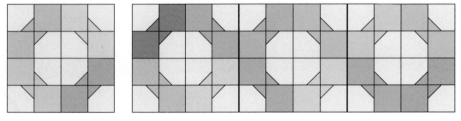

Row Assembly Diagram

5. One at a time, pick up blocks around edge of quilt. Referring to photo, join navy Y triangles to all block corners that will abut border (2 corners on all except 4 corner blocks, which need 3 navy triangles). For A blocks, join Y triangles to dark X triangles. For B blocks, join Y triangles to light X triangles. Return blocks to layout and recheck position.

6. One at a time, pick up blocks in each row and add light/medium Y triangles to remaining corners. Square up completed blocks to 8" x 8".

7. Join blocks in each row. Press seam allowances in opposite directions from row to row.

8. Join rows.

ADDING BORDERS

1. Read instructions for mitered borders on pages 150 and 151.

2. Measure length of quilt; then mark both longer borders to match length. Measure width of quilt and mark 2 remaining borders to match width. Join borders to quilt. Press seam allowances toward borders. Miter corners.

3. If you want rounded corners, use a large dinner plate (about 14" diameter) for a template. Center plate over mitered seam at each corner and mark curve. Do not cut fabric until after quilting is finished.

FINISHING

1. Divide backing fabric into 2 (3-yard) lengths. Cut 1 piece in half lengthwise. Sew a narrow panel to each side of wide panel. Press seam allowances toward narrow panels.

2. Select a cable or other suitable design for border. Mark desired quilting designs on quilt top.

3. Layer backing, batting, and quilt top. Baste. Quilt as desired. On quilt shown, patchwork is outline-quilted.

4. Make 10½ yards of bias or straight-grain binding. See pages 158 and 159 for instructions on making and applying binding. Make bias binding for rounded corners, and stitch binding to drawn outline of each corner. Trim excess fabric from rounded corners before turning binding to backing.

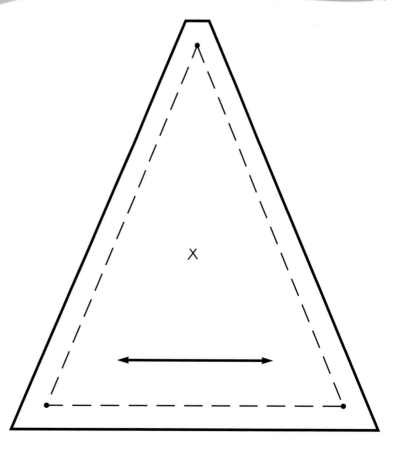

VARIABLE SIZES			
Size	Wall/Crib	Twin	King
Finished Size	42" x 49½"	68½" x 91"	98½" x 98½"
Number of Blocks	20	70	121
Blocks Set	4 x 5	7 x 10	11 x 11
Border Width (finished size)	6"	8"	8"

X

MATERIALS

for finished size 84" x 99"*

For 99 blocks:

66 (4¾" x 10") light-valued scraps

66 (4¾" x 10") medium-valued scraps

66 (4¾" x 10") dark-valued scraps

40 (6") squares of light and medium value

For borders and binding:

4 yards navy fabric

6 yards backing fabric or 3 yards 108"-wide muslin

90" x 108" precut batting

This quilt fits a double or queen bed. Requirements for other sizes are listed on page 26.

CUTTING

Cut all strips cross-grain unless stated otherwise.

Instructions are given for either rotary cutting or cutting with templates. A pattern for Triangle X is on page 26.

From 4¾" x 10" scraps, cut:

• 792 of Template X.

If you prefer to cut without using a template, see Cutting Diagram for cutting measurements.

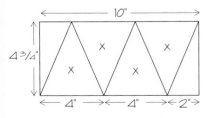

Cutting Diagram

From *each* 6" square, cut:

• 4 (3") squares. Cut each square in half diagonally to get 320 Y triangles.

From navy fabric, cut:

• 1 (32") square for bias binding or 9 (2½"-wide) strips for straight-grain binding. (Decide whether you want square or rounded corners before cutting binding. See Finishing, Step 4.)

• 2 (8½" x 103") lengthwise strips and 2 (8½" x 90") lengthwise strips for border.

• 38 (3") squares. Cut each square in half diagonally to get 76 Y triangles.

QUILT TOP ASSEMBLY

Finished size of block is 7½" square.

1. For each block, select 4 dark X triangles and 4 light or medium X triangles. Join each dark triangle to a light or medium triangle (Block Assembly Diagram). Press seam allowances toward dark triangles.

2. Join 2 pairs of X triangles to make each half-block, joining light fabric to dark fabric (Block Assembly Diagram). Join half-blocks. Press all seam allowances in same direction.

3. Make 99 blocks in this manner.

4. Once you decide which block goes where, then you'll know how to add Y triangles to each block. This quilt is a straight set, with blocks set 9 x 11 (see setting illustration on page 149). Lay out blocks in 11 horizontal rows, with 9 blocks in each row. Turn first block in Row 1 (Row Assembly Diagram) to put dark X triangles at corners (Block A Diagram); then turn next block to place light X triangles at corners (Block B Diagram). Fill out row with 7 more blocks, alternating A and B positions as shown. Lay out Row 2 in same manner, starting with a B block and alternating A and B positions. Lay out 11 rows, alternating rows 1 and 2 as shown in photo on page 27. Rearrange blocks until satisfied with placement. (Continued)

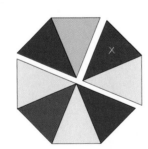

Block Assembly Diagram

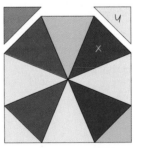

Block A Diagram

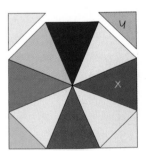

Block B Diagram

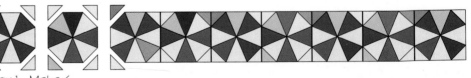

Row 1—Make 6.

Row 2—Make 5.

Row Assembly Diagram

Quilt by Mimi Alef of High Point, North Carolina

BUTTERFLIES

This easy and elegant appliquéd quilt is inspired by a 1930s classic. Turn the blocks this way and that to make the butterflies flit and fly in different directions.

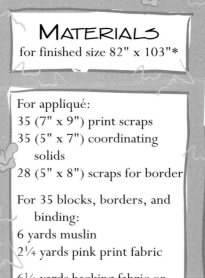

MATERIALS
for finished size 82" x 103"*

For appliqué:
35 (7" x 9") print scraps
35 (5" x 7") coordinating
    solids
28 (5" x 8") scraps for border

For 35 blocks, borders, and
    binding:
6 yards muslin
2¼ yards pink print fabric
6¼ yards backing fabric or
    3⅛ yards 90"-wide
    muslin
90" x 108" precut batting
Assorted embroidery floss
Nonpermanent fabric marker

*This quilt fits a double or queen bed. Requirements for other sizes are listed on page 30.

CUTTING

Before cutting, choose an appliqué technique. Directions on cutting pieces for hand appliqué are on page 144. Make templates for patterns A–F on page 32. Add seam allowances when cutting fabric.

Cut all strips cross-grain unless stated otherwise.

From 7" x 9" scraps, cut:
• 35 A wings.
• 35 A rev. wings.
• 35 C bodies.

From 5" x 7" scraps, cut:
• 35 B wings.
• 35 B rev. wings.

From 5" x 8" scraps, cut:
• 28 D wings.
• 28 D rev. wings.
• 28 E wings.
• 28 E rev. wings.
• 28 F bodies.

From muslin, cut:
• 2 (6½" x 103") lengthwise strips and
  2 (6½" x 80") lengthwise strips for
  middle border.
• 1 (16" x 56") rectangle for bias binding or 7 (2½" x 56") lengthwise strips
  for straight-grain binding.
• 35 (11¼") squares.

From pink print, cut:
• 17 (4¼"-wide) strips for inner and
  outer borders.

MAKING BLOCKS

Finished size of block is 10¾" square.
1. For each block, select 1 muslin square, 1 A wing, 1 A rev. wing, 1 B wing, 1 B rev. wing, and 1 C body. Prepare wings and body for appliqué.

Directions on preparing pieces for hand appliqué are on page 147.
2. Fold each square in half diagonally in both directions, finger-pressing creases for placement guides.
3. Place muslin square over large butterfly pattern, matching center of square with center mark on pattern. Lightly trace antennae and butterfly outline onto muslin.
4. Position A and A rev. wings on muslin and appliqué. Stitch B and B rev. wings; then appliqué C body. Complete appliqué for 35 blocks.
5. Use 2 strands of embroidery floss to outline-stitch antennae. Embroidery stitch diagrams are on page 135.

JOINING BLOCKS

This quilt is an example of a straight set, with the blocks set 5 x 7. See setting illustration on page 149.
1. Lay out blocks in 7 horizontal rows, with 5 blocks in each row (Row Assembly Diagram). Make 4 of Row 1 and 3 of Row 2. When satisfied with placement, join blocks in each row.
2. Join rows, alternating rows as shown in photo. (Continued)

Row 1—Make 4.

Row 2—Make 3.

Row Assembly Diagram

MAKING APPLIQUÉD BORDER

1. Fold 4 muslin border strips in half and lightly mark a center line.

2. Starting at center line of 1 long strip, mark additional placement lines every 10¾" along length of border strip until you have 7 evenly spaced lines (*Border Diagram*). On each line, measure 3¼" from raw edge and mark midpoint of line. Repeat for second long border strip. There will be extra fabric on strip ends for mitered corners.

3. Mark 2 shorter border strips in same manner, measuring 10¾" segments from centers until you have 5 evenly spaced lines.

4. Place 1 muslin strip over small butterfly pattern, matching 1 placement line with marked center of pattern. Trace antennae and outline of butterfly onto muslin. Repeat, centering traced butterflies over each marked line on border. In this manner, trace butterflies on all 4 border strips.

5. Select 1 D wing, 1 D rev. wing, 1 E wing, 1 E rev. wing, and 1 F body for each border butterfly. Prepare wings and bodies for appliqué.

6. For each butterfly, place D and D rev. wings on muslin and appliqué. Stitch E and E rev. wings; then appliqué F body.

7. Embroider antennae.

ADDING BORDERS

1. Read instructions for mitered borders on pages 150 and 151.

2. Join 2 pink border strips end-to-end for each side of quilt. Measure length of quilt; then mark 2 borders to match length. Measure width of quilt and mark 2 remaining borders to match width. Join borders to quilt. Press seam allowances toward borders. Miter corners.

3. In same manner, join muslin borders to quilt and miter corners. Press seam allowances toward borders. Repeat to add pink outer borders.

4. Center each corner seam of muslin borders over small butterfly pattern and trace outline of butterfly onto muslin. Appliqué a butterfly at each corner.

FINISHING

1. Divide backing fabric into 2 (3⅛-yard) lengths. Cut 1 piece in half lengthwise. Sew a narrow panel to each side of wide panel. Press seam allowances toward narrow panels.

2. An upside-down butterfly is quilted between appliquéd butterflies in muslin border. See page 154 for tips on making a quilting stencil of small butterfly pattern. A pattern for heart quilted in block corners is below. Select a cable or other suitable design for pink borders. Mark desired quilting designs on quilt top.

3. Layer backing, batting, and quilt top. Baste. Quilt as desired. On quilt shown, butterflies are echo-quilted.

4. Make 10¾ yards of bias or straight-grain binding. See pages 158 and 159 for instructions on making and applying binding.

|← 10¾" →|← 10¾" →|← 10¾" →|← 10¾" →|← 10¾" →|← 10¾" →|

Border Diagram

VARIABLE SIZES

Size	Wall/Crib	Twin	King
Finished Size	41½" x 52"	71" x 92½"	103" x 103"
Number of Blocks	6	24	49
Blocks Set	2 x 3	4 x 6	7 x 7
Border Widths (finished size)	4", 6"	4", 6", 4"	4", 6", 4"
Number of Border Butterflies	14	24	32

Heart Quilting Pattern

Quilt by Dorothy Cowell Servis of Columbus, New Jersey

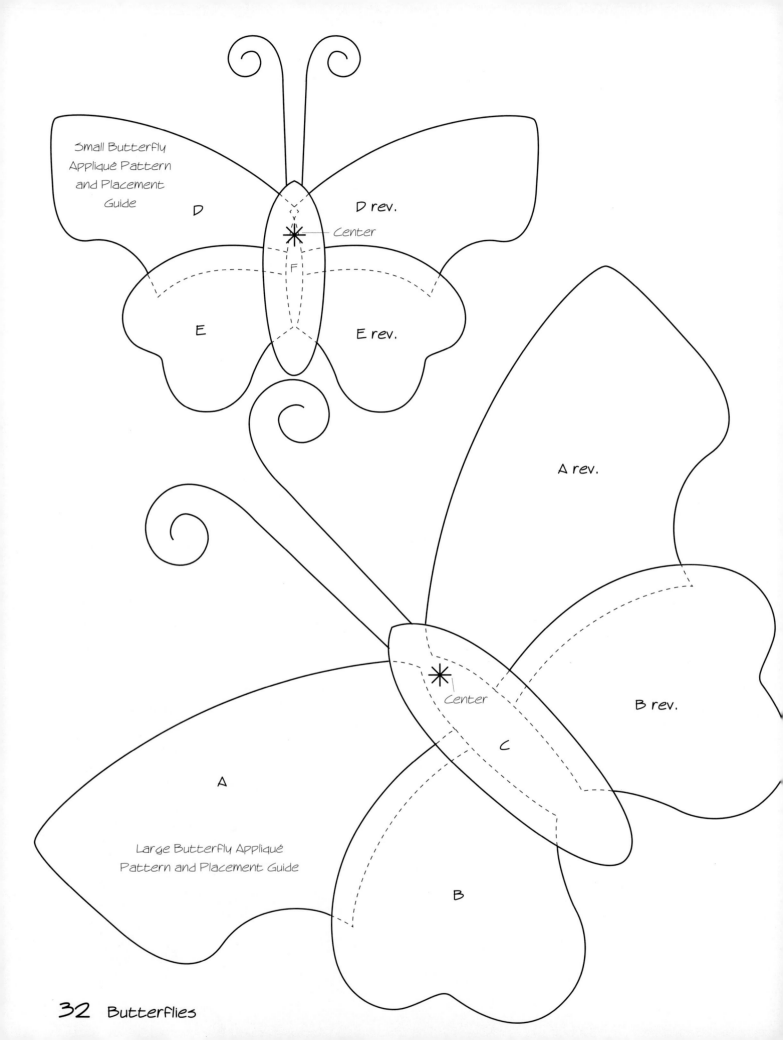

Small Butterfly
Appliqué Pattern
and Placement
Guide

D

D rev.

Center

F

E

E rev.

A rev.

A

B rev.

C

Large Butterfly Appliqué
Pattern and Placement Guide

Center

B

TENDER LOVING CARE

We all want to proudly display our quilts, but they must be protected from harmful elements to preserve them.

Quilts should be shielded from direct light and heat, dust, damp, cigarette smoke, and aerosol sprays. The following suggestions for display, storage, and cleaning are suitable for most quilts. A museum-quality heirloom has special needs; if you have such a quilt, get expert advice on its care.

Washing Up

Any quilt that is really used will need to be cleaned. You can wash a quilt if fabrics were prewashed and tested for colorfastness before the quilt was made. When in doubt, test a corner of the quilt to be sure dyes do not bleed.

Some people trust today's fabrics enough to toss a quilt in a large-capacity washing machine with the rest of the laundry. Others prefer to wash a quilt by hand in a tub. Follow these tips to wash your quilt safely.

• Use a mild soap in cold water. Never use bleach. Many experts recommend Orvis Paste, an all-natural soap originally developed for washing animals. Free of chemicals found in detergents, a single spoonful of Orvis Paste cleans a quilt nicely. This soap is available at many quilt shops, farm supply stores, and from several mail-order catalogs.

• The heat and agitation of a dryer really takes the life out of fabric, so air drying is best. Dry a wet quilt by laying it flat on the floor or outside on the grass on clean towels. A wet quilt is very heavy, so be sure to gently squeeze out excess water; then lift and carry it in a way that avoids putting stress on the seams.

• Dry cleaning is not advisable because the chemicals in commercial cleaning fluids can be harmful.

Fading Away

Exposure to light takes a toll on fabric, so all quilts fade to some degree over time. Some fabrics fade faster and more drastically than others, and there is no sure way to identify these fabrics beforehand. However, here is a simple test that is worthwhile if you have time.

Cut a 4" square of each prewashed fabric and tape the squares to a sunny window. After 15 days, compare the squares to the remaining yardage. If the squares of fabric have faded to the same degree, you can assume the finished quilt will keep a uniform appearance as it ages. If one fabric fades more than the others, however, you might want to select another for your quilt.

A Breath of Air

By changing the quilt on your bed regularly, no one quilt is exposed for long. Rotate quilts with the change of each season, for their own good as well as a fresh look.

All quilts collect dust. Before you put a quilt away for the season, shake it and air it outdoors. A breezy, overcast day is best if the humidity is low. Lay towels on the grass or over a railing; then spread the quilt over the towels. Keep the quilt out of direct sunlight.

Tucked Away

Store your quilts in a cool, dry place, each in its own wrapping. Winter cold and summer heat make attics and garages inappropriate storage areas. Basements are off-limits, too, if there is the slightest risk of dampness.

Wrap each quilt in a cotton sheet, pillowcase, or in acid-free tissue paper. Boxes made of acid-free material are also available. Crumpled paper placed inside each fold prevents stains from developing along fold lines. These materials let air circulate but still protect the quilt from dust and damp. *Do not store quilts in plastic,* which traps moisture and encourages the growth of mildew.

If you keep your quilt on a rack or in a chest, put several layers of acid-free paper or muslin between the quilt and the wood. A quilt should not be in contact with wood for a long time, as the natural acids in wood will eventually stain the cloth.

Each time you put a quilt away, fold it differently to prevent damage where fabric fibers become cracked and weak. If possible, avoid folds altogether by rolling the quilt around a tube or cotton towel.

BUCKEYE BEAUTY

A quick-piecing method for triangle-squares makes this quilt easy to make.
Joined in a straight set, the blocks melt together and create an overall design
of diamonds twinkling between crisscrossing patchwork chains.

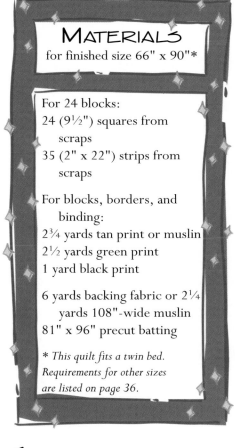

MATERIALS
for finished size 66" x 90"*

For 24 blocks:
24 (9½") squares from
    scraps
35 (2" x 22") strips from
    scraps

For blocks, borders, and
    binding:
2¾ yards tan print or muslin
2½ yards green print
1 yard black print

6 yards backing fabric or 2¼
    yards 108"-wide muslin
81" x 96" precut batting

*This quilt fits a twin bed.
Requirements for other sizes
are listed on page 36.*

CUTTING
Cut all strips cross-grain unless stated
otherwise.

From tan fabric, cut:
• 24 (9½") squares.
• 35 (2" x 22") strips.

From green print fabric, cut:
• 2 (3" x 56") lengthwise strips and 2
    (3" x 75") lengthwise strips for inner
    border.
• 2 (4" x 69") lengthwise strips and 2
    (4" x 86") lengthwise strips for outer
    border.

• 2 (14") squares for bias binding or 4
    (2½" x 86") lengthwise strips for
    straight-grain binding.
    Note: If desired, add remaining fabric
    to scraps for patchwork.

From black print fabric, cut:
• 8 (3½" x 44") strips for middle border.

MAKING BLOCKS
Finished size of block is 12" square.
1. On wrong side of each tan square,
mark 4 (3⅞") squares (Diagram A), leaving a small margin of fabric around
drawing. Draw diagonal lines through
squares as shown.
2. With right sides facing, match 1
marked square with a scrap square. Stitch
¼" seam on *both* sides of diagonal lines
(Diagram B). Press. Cut on all drawn lines
to get 8 triangle-squares. Repeat with all
tan and scrap squares to get a total of 192
triangle-squares. Press seam allowances

toward scrap fabric; then trim points of
seam allowances. Each triangle-square
should be 3½" square.
3. Join each 2" x 22" tan strip to 1
scrap strip (Diagram C). Press seam
allowances toward scrap fabrics. Rotary-
cut 11 (2"-wide) segments from each
strip set to get a total of 384 segments
(and 1 extra).
4. Select 2 segments at random and
join to make a four-patch (Diagram D).
Make 192 four-patches, 8 for each
block. Each four-patch should be 3½"
square.
5. Join 1 triangle-square to each four-
patch (Diagram E), positioning units as
shown. (It's easy to get the four-patch
turned around, so be careful.) Press
seam allowances toward triangle-
squares. Then join units in pairs as
shown to make 96 quarter sections.

(Continued)

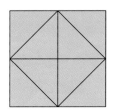

Diagram A

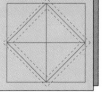

Diagram B

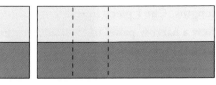

Diagram C

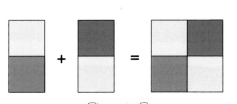

Diagram D

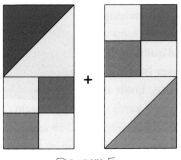

Diagram E

GUSSIE GROAT'S BONNET

This quilt was three generations in the making. Gussie Groat made 20 blocks in the 1920s, stitching the pieces together with a running stitch of black floss. Gussie's primitive-style girls were joined together and quilted 60 years later by her grandson's wife, Maria Groat.

MATERIALS
for finished size 56" x 84"*

For 24 blocks:
2¾ yards muslin
24 (6" x 9") assorted prints
24 (6" x 7") assorted solids
96 (1¾" x 12") scrap strips
96 (1¾") scrap squares

⅞ yard binding fabric
3½ yards backing fabric or
   1¾ yards 90"-wide muslin
72" x 90" precut batting
Nonpermanent fabric marker
Black embroidery floss

This quilt fits a twin bed. Requirements for other sizes are listed on page 40.

CUTTING

Before cutting, choose an appliqué technique. Directions on cutting pieces for hand appliqué are on page 144. Make templates for patterns A–E on page 41. Add seam allowance when cutting fabric.

Cut all strips cross-grain unless stated otherwise.

From *each* print scrap, cut:
• 1 of Template B.

From *each* solid scrap, cut:
• 1 each of templates A, C, and E.

From muslin, cut:
• 24 (12") squares.
• 24 of Template D.

From binding fabric, cut:
• 1 (31") square for bias binding or 7 (2½"-wide) strips for straight-grain binding.

MAKING BLOCKS

Finished size of block is 14" square.

1. Fold each muslin square in half diagonally, vertically, and horizontally, finger-pressing a crease in each direction for placement guides. Position square over pattern, matching center of square with marked center of pattern. Lightly trace outline of pattern onto square.

2. For each block, select A, C, and E pieces of the same fabric, and 1 each of pieces B and D. Prepare pieces A, B, C, and D for appliqué. Directions on preparing pieces for hand appliqué are on page 147.

3. Position A (shoe) on square and appliqué. Position B (dress) and C (bonnet). Appliqué.

4. Turn under the "cuff" edge of E (arm) and stitch it to D (hand). Turn under outer edges of combined unit; then appliqué unit in place on dress.

5. Complete appliqué for 24 blocks. If desired, use 3 strands of floss to work a small running stitch around outside edge of each piece as shown on pattern.

6. Select 4 scrap strips and 4 squares for each block. Sew squares to ends of 2 strips. Press seam allowances toward strips. Join 2 plain strips to sides of block (*Block Assembly Diagram*). Press seam allowances toward strips. Join strips with squares to top and bottom edges of block. Complete 24 blocks.

Block Assembly Diagram

JOINING BLOCKS

This quilt is an example of a straight set, with the blocks set 4 x 6. See setting illustration on page 149.

1. Lay out blocks in 6 horizontal rows, with 4 blocks in each row (*Row Assembly Diagram*). When satisfied with placement, join blocks in each row.

2. Join rows. (Continued)

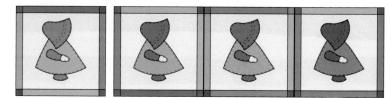

Row Assembly Diagram

BUCKEYE BEAUTY

A quick-piecing method for triangle-squares makes this quilt easy to make.
Joined in a straight set, the blocks melt together and create an overall design
of diamonds twinkling between crisscrossing patchwork chains.

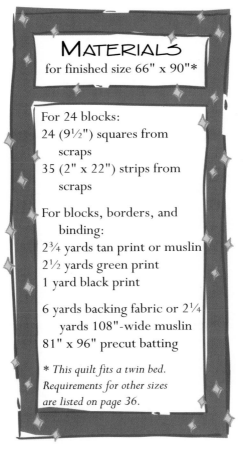

MATERIALS
for finished size 66" x 90"*

For 24 blocks:
24 (9½") squares from
   scraps
35 (2" x 22") strips from
   scraps

For blocks, borders, and
   binding:
2¾ yards tan print or muslin
2½ yards green print
1 yard black print

6 yards backing fabric or 2¼
   yards 108"-wide muslin
81" x 96" precut batting

*This quilt fits a twin bed.
Requirements for other sizes
are listed on page 36.*

CUTTING

Cut all strips cross-grain unless stated
otherwise.

From tan fabric, cut:
• 24 (9½") squares.
• 35 (2" x 22") strips.

From green print fabric, cut:
• 2 (3" x 56") lengthwise strips and 2
(3" x 75") lengthwise strips for inner
border.
• 2 (4" x 69") lengthwise strips and 2
(4" x 86") lengthwise strips for outer
border.

• 2 (14") squares for bias binding or 4
(2½" x 86") lengthwise strips for
straight-grain binding.
Note: If desired, add remaining fabric
to scraps for patchwork.

From black print fabric, cut:
• 8 (3½" x 44") strips for middle border.

MAKING BLOCKS

Finished size of block is 12" square.
1. On wrong side of each tan square,
mark 4 (3⅞") squares (Diagram A), leaving a small margin of fabric around
drawing. Draw diagonal lines through
squares as shown.
2. With right sides facing, match 1
marked square with a scrap square. Stitch
¼" seam on *both* sides of diagonal lines
(Diagram B). Press. Cut on all drawn lines
to get 8 triangle-squares. Repeat with all
tan and scrap squares to get a total of 192
triangle-squares. Press seam allowances

toward scrap fabric; then trim points of
seam allowances. Each triangle-square
should be 3½" square.
3. Join each 2" x 22" tan strip to 1
scrap strip (Diagram C). Press seam
allowances toward scrap fabrics. Rotary-
cut 11 (2"-wide) segments from each
strip set to get a total of 384 segments
(and 1 extra).
4. Select 2 segments at random and
join to make a four-patch (Diagram D).
Make 192 four-patches, 8 for each
block. Each four-patch should be 3½"
square.
5. Join 1 triangle-square to each four-
patch (Diagram E), positioning units as
shown. (It's easy to get the four-patch
turned around, so be careful.) Press
seam allowances toward triangle-
squares. Then join units in pairs as
shown to make 96 quarter sections.

(Continued)

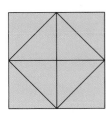

Diagram A

Diagram B

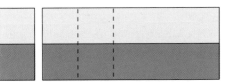

Diagram C

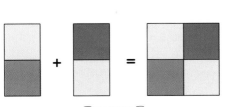

Diagram D

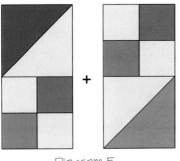

Diagram E

6. For each block, join quarter sections in 2 rows (*Block Assembly Diagram*). Join rows to complete block.

7. Make 24 blocks. Square up blocks to 12½" x 12½".

JOINING BLOCKS

This quilt is an example of a straight set, with the blocks set 4 x 6. See setting illustration on page 149.

1. Lay out blocks in 6 horizontal rows, with 4 blocks in each row (*Row Assembly Diagram*). When satisfied with placement, join blocks in each row.

2. Join rows as shown in photo.

ADDING BORDERS

1. Referring to instructions on page 150, measure quilt; then trim 2 (3" x 75") green print borders to match length. Join borders to quilt sides. Press seam allowances toward borders.

2. Measure quilt width and trim 2 (56") green print borders to match. Join borders to quilt top and bottom.

3. For middle border, join 2 black print border strips end-to-end for each side of quilt. Repeat steps 1 and 2 to join borders to quilt top.

4. For outer border, trim remaining green print strips to fit. Join borders to quilt top.

FINISHING

1. Divide backing fabric into 2 (3-yard) lengths. Cut 1 piece in half lengthwise. Sew a narrow panel to each side of wide panel. Press seam allowances toward narrow panels.

2. On quilt shown, patchwork and borders are outline-quilted. Two alternative quilting designs are shown (*Alternate Quilting Diagrams*). Mark desired quilting designs on quilt top.

3. Layer backing, batting, and quilt top. Baste. Quilt as desired.

4. Make 9 yards of bias or straight-grain binding. See pages 158 and 159 for instructions on making and applying binding.

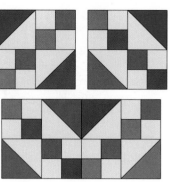

Block Assembly Diagram

Row Assembly Diagram

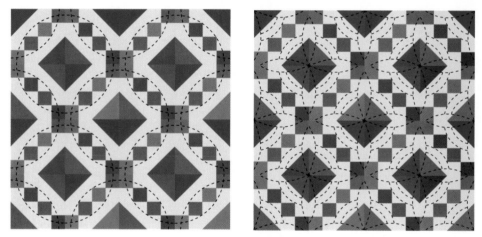

Alternate Quilting Diagrams

VARIABLE SIZES

Size	Wall/Crib	Double/Queen	King
Finished Size	43" x 43"	90" x 102"	108" x 108"
Number of Blocks	9	42	49
Blocks Set	3 x 3	6 x 7	7 x 7
Border Widths (finished size)	1", 2½"	2½", 3", 3½"	3", 4", 5"

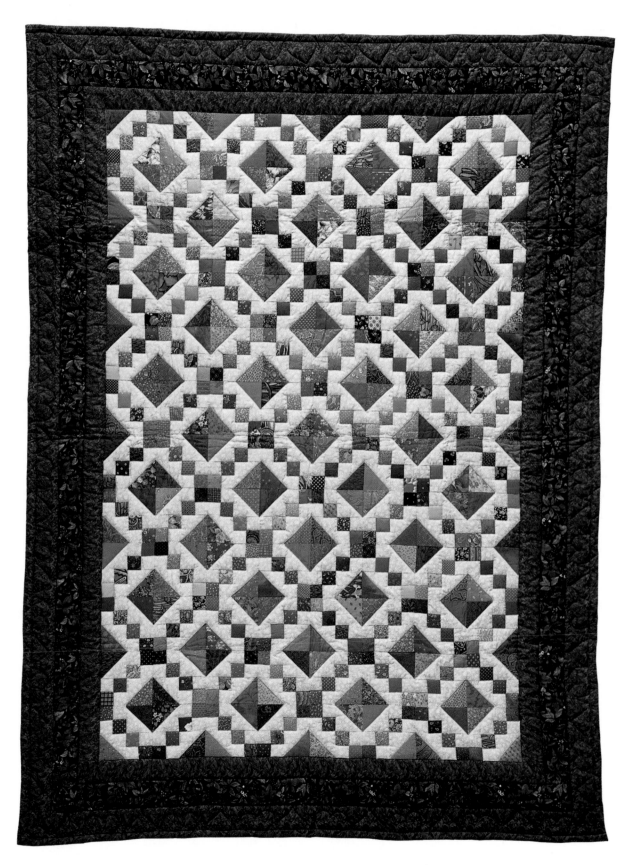

Quilt by Helen Johnstone of Glendora, New Jersey

Buckeye Beauty **37**

GUSSIE GROAT'S BONNET

This quilt was three generations in the making. Gussie Groat made 20 blocks in the 1920s, stitching the pieces together with a running stitch of black floss. Gussie's primitive-style girls were joined together and quilted 60 years later by her grandson's wife, Maria Groat.

MATERIALS
for finished size 56" x 84"*

For 24 blocks:
2¾ yards muslin
24 (6" x 9") assorted prints
24 (6" x 7") assorted solids
96 (1¼" x 12") scrap strips
96 (1¼") scrap squares

⅞ yard binding fabric
3½ yards backing fabric or
   1¾ yards 90"-wide muslin
72" x 90" precut batting
Nonpermanent fabric marker
Black embroidery floss

This quilt fits a twin bed. Requirements for other sizes are listed on page 40.

CUTTING
Before cutting, choose an appliqué technique. Directions on cutting pieces for hand appliqué are on page 144. Make templates for patterns A–E on page 41. Add seam allowance when cutting fabric.
  Cut all strips cross-grain unless stated otherwise.

From *each* print scrap, cut:
• 1 of Template B.

From *each* solid scrap, cut:
• 1 each of templates A, C, and E.

From muslin, cut:
• 24 (12") squares.
• 24 of Template D.

From binding fabric, cut:
• 1 (31") square for bias binding or 7 (2½"-wide) strips for straight-grain binding.

MAKING BLOCKS
Finished size of block is 14" square.
1. Fold each muslin square in half diagonally, vertically, and horizontally, finger-pressing a crease in each direction for placement guides. Position square over pattern, matching center of square with marked center of pattern. Lightly trace outline of pattern onto square.
2. For each block, select A, C, and E pieces of the same fabric, and 1 each of pieces B and D. Prepare pieces A, B, C, and D for appliqué. Directions on preparing pieces for hand appliqué are on page 147.
3. Position A (shoe) on square and appliqué. Position B (dress) and C (bonnet). Appliqué.
4. Turn under the "cuff" edge of E (arm) and stitch it to D (hand). Turn under outer edges of combined unit; then appliqué unit in place on dress.

5. Complete appliqué for 24 blocks. If desired, use 3 strands of floss to work a small running stitch around outside edge of each piece as shown on pattern.
6. Select 4 scrap strips and 4 squares for each block. Sew squares to ends of 2 strips. Press seam allowances toward strips. Join 2 plain strips to sides of block (*Block Assembly Diagram*). Press seam allowances toward strips. Join strips with squares to top and bottom edges of block. Complete 24 blocks.

Block Assembly Diagram

JOINING BLOCKS
This quilt is an example of a straight set, with the blocks set 4 x 6. See setting illustration on page 149.
1. Lay out blocks in 6 horizontal rows, with 4 blocks in each row (*Row Assembly Diagram*). When satisfied with placement, join blocks in each row.
2. Join rows. *(Continued)*

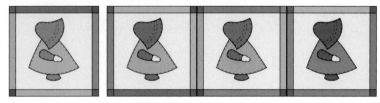

Row Assembly Diagram

FINISHING

1. Divide backing fabric into 2 (1¾-yard) lengths. Cut 1 piece in half lengthwise. Sew a narrow panel to each side of wide panel. Press seam allowances toward narrow panels.

2. On quilt shown, girls are outline-quilted and lines of cross-hatching, spaced 1" apart, are quilted in the muslin. Mark desired quilting designs on quilt top.

3. Layer backing, batting, and quilt top. Baste. Quilt as desired.

4. Make 8 yards of bias or straight-grain binding. See pages 158 and 159 for instructions on making and applying binding.

Quilt by the late Augusta Groat and by Maria Groat of Bainbridge Island, Washington

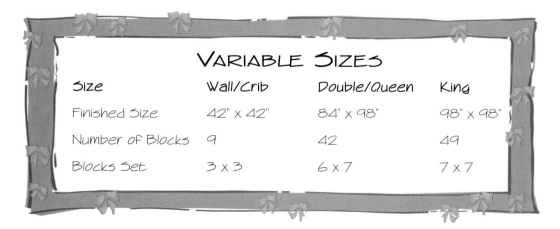

VARIABLE SIZES

Size	Wall/Crib	Double/Queen	King
Finished Size	42" x 42"	84" x 98"	98" x 98"
Number of Blocks	9	42	49
Blocks Set	3 x 3	6 x 7	7 x 7

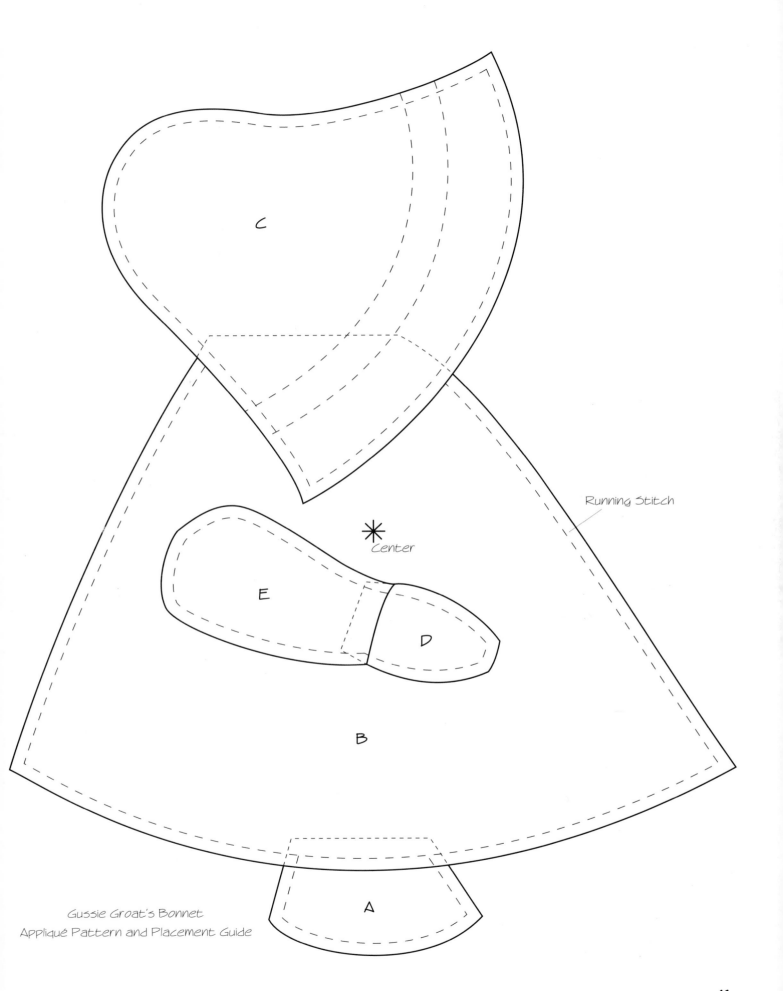

C

Running Stitch

✳ Center

E

D

B

A

Gussie Groat's Bonnet
Appliqué Pattern and Placement Guide

BARN RAISING LOG CABIN

Play with color value to make this classic quilt. Deciding which fabrics are "light" and which are "dark" is fun—pink, gold, and mint join cream and tan on the light side, while bright and moody fabrics blend on the dark side. Mediums can go either way.

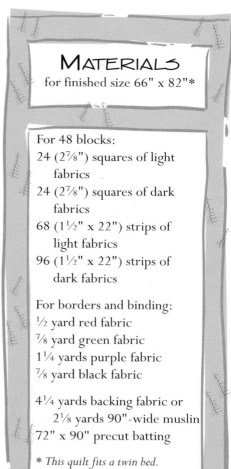

MATERIALS
for finished size 66" x 82"*

For 48 blocks:
24 (2⅞") squares of light fabrics
24 (2⅞") squares of dark fabrics
68 (1½" x 22") strips of light fabrics
96 (1½" x 22") strips of dark fabrics

For borders and binding:
½ yard red fabric
⅞ yard green fabric
1¼ yards purple fabric
⅞ yard black fabric

4¼ yards backing fabric or
    2⅛ yards 90"-wide muslin
72" x 90" precut batting

* This quilt fits a twin bed. Requirements for other sizes are listed on page 44.

CUTTING
Cut all strips cross-grain.

Note: Yardage given for strips is a guideline that assumes 1 strip will make 3 or 4 logs scattered throughout the quilt. Because you're using small bits of fabric for individual logs, you can cut as many scraps as you like, each 1½" wide.

From red fabric, cut:
• 8 (2"-wide) strips for inner border.

From green fabric, cut:
• 8 (3½"-wide) strips for middle border.

From purple fabric, cut:
• 8 (5"-wide) strips for outer border.

From black fabric, cut:
• 1 (30") square for bias binding or 8 (2½"-wide) strips for straight-grain binding.

MAKING BLOCKS
Finished size of block is 8" square.

1. Unlike a traditional Log Cabin block with its solid center square, this block's center is pieced from 2 triangles. To get 96 triangles, cut each 2⅞" square in half diagonally. Sort them into light/dark pairs; then join triangles to make 48 triangle-squares (Diagram A). Press seam allowances toward dark fabric.

2. To start 1 block, select 1 light strip for first log. With right sides facing, match strip to light side of 1 triangle-square as shown and stitch (Diagram B). Trim log even with bottom of triangle-square. Press seam allowance toward new log.

3. Turn unit so new log is at top. With right sides facing, match another light strip to remaining light edge of triangle-square and stitch (Diagram C). Trim new log even with bottom of unit as before. Press seam allowance toward new log.

4. Turn unit so new log is at top. With right sides facing, match a dark strip to dark edge of triangle-square and stitch (Diagram D). Trim log even with bottom of unit and press. (Continued)

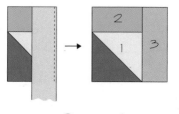

Diagram A

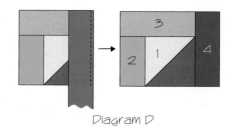

Diagram B

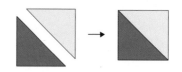

Diagram C

Diagram D

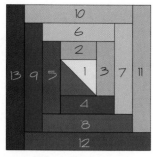

Block Diagram

5. Continue adding logs in this manner until you have 3 logs on all sides of center triangle-square (Block Diagram). Always press seam allowances toward newest log; then rotate unit to put new log at top edge to add next strip.

6. Make 48 blocks. Square up blocks to 8½" x 8½".

JOINING BLOCKS

This quilt is an example of a straight set, with the blocks set 6 x 8. See setting illustration on page 149.

1. For top half of quilt, lay out blocks in 4 horizontal rows with 6 blocks in each row (Row Assembly Diagram). Note that you're always matching a light edge to a light edge and dark to dark. Turn diagram upside down and repeat to lay out 4 more rows for bottom half of quilt. When satisfied with placement, join blocks in each row. Press seam allowances in different directions from row to row.

2. Lay out all rows, checking block placement against diagrams and photo. Join rows.

ADDING BORDERS

1. Join 2 (2"-wide) red strips for each inner side border. Referring to instructions on page 150, measure quilt from top to bottom; then trim borders to match length. Join borders to quilt sides. Press seam allowances toward borders.

2. Join 2 red strips for top border. Measure quilt from side to side; then trim border to match quilt width. Join border to quilt top. Repeat for bottom border.

3. Join pairs of 3½"-wide green strips for middle borders. Measure length of

quilt and trim 2 border strips to fit; join borders to quilt. Measure and sew top and bottom borders in same manner.

4. Join pairs of 5"-wide purple strips for outer border. Join borders to quilt as for middle border.

FINISHING

1. Divide backing fabric into 2 (2⅛-yard) lengths. Cut 1 piece in half lengthwise. Sew a narrow panel to each side of wide panel. Press seam allowances toward narrow panels.

2. On quilt shown, rows of concentric half-circles swirl across the patchwork and into the inner border. Select appropriate designs for middle and outer borders. Mark quilting designs on quilt top.

3. Layer backing, batting, and quilt top. Backing seam should be parallel with top and bottom edges. Baste. Quilt as desired.

4. Make 8½ yards of bias or straight-grain binding. See pages 158 and 159 for instructions on making and applying binding.

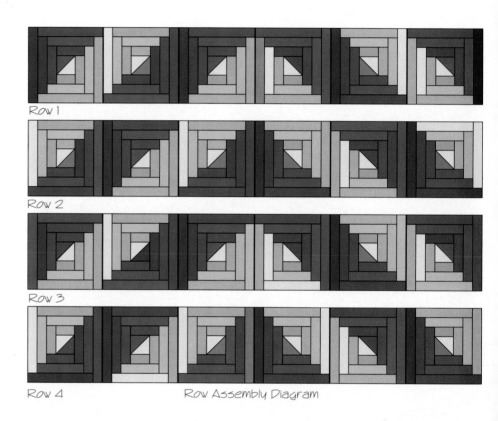

Row 1

Row 2

Row 3

Row 4　　　　Row Assembly Diagram

VARIABLE SIZES

Size	Wall/Crib	Double/Queen	King
Finished Size	41" x 41"	86" x 102"	102" x 102"
Number of Blocks	16	80	100
Blocks Set	4 x 4	8 x 10	10 x 10
Border Widths (Finished size)	1½", 3"	2", 3½", 5½"	2", 3½", 5½"

Quilt by Lila Taylor Scott of Marietta, Georgia

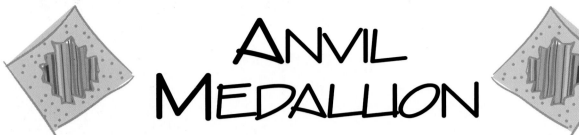

ANVIL MEDALLION

Have a passion for plaids? Mix them with prints, stripes, or with each other
in these quick-pieced blocks, presented in a dynamic diagonal medallion setting.
Note that some blocks have high contrast, others don't.

MATERIALS
for finished size 80" x 108"*

For 50 blocks:
50 (6" x 25") dark scraps
50 (5" x 25") light scraps

For setting triangles, borders, and binding:
½ yard gold fabric
1¾ yards yellow plaid
3 yards navy small plaid
¼ yard navy large plaid

6½ yards backing or 3¼
   yards 90"-wide muslin
120" x 120" precut batting

*This quilt fits a double or queen
bed. Requirements for other sizes
are listed on page 50.*

CUTTING
Cut all strips cross-grain unless stated
otherwise.

From *each* dark scrap, cut:
• 1 (5½") square.
• 1 (5" x 18") strip for triangle-squares.

From *each* light scrap, cut:
• 2 (3") squares.
• 1 (5" x 18") strip for triangle-squares.

From gold fabric, cut:
• 20 (5½") squares.

From yellow plaid, cut:
• 1 (33") square for bias binding or 10
  (2½"-wide) strips for straight-grain
  binding.
• 10 (8¼") squares.
  Cut each square in quarters diagonally
  to get 4 triangles, a total of 40 triangles.
• 2 (8") squares.
  Cut each square in half diagonally to
  get a total of 4 corner triangles.

From navy small plaid, cut:
• 2 (5½" x 103") lengthwise strips and
  2 (5½" x 75") lengthwise strips for
  border.
• 4 (5½" x 42") lengthwise strips for
  medallion.
  *Note: If desired, use remaining fabric
  for blocks.*

From navy large plaid, cut:
• 8 (5½") squares for border corners.

MAKING BLOCKS
Finished size of block is 10" square.
1. Select 1 light fabric and 1 dark fabric
for each block.
2. On wrong side of 5" x 18" light
scrap, mark a row of 5 (3⅜") squares
(Diagram A), leaving a small margin of
fabric around drawing. Draw diagonal
lines through squares as shown.
3. With right sides facing, match marked
light scrap with its dark partner. Stitch ¼"
seam on *both* sides of diagonal lines, pivoting at corners to sew continuously from
start to finish (Diagram B). Press. Cut on
all drawn lines to get 10 triangle-squares.
Press seam allowances toward dark fabric.

4. Join triangle-squares in 2 rows of 3
and 2 rows of 2 (Block Assembly
Diagram), always matching dark triangle
to light triangle. Press seam allowances
toward dark fabric.
5. Join 2-square rows to sides of 5½"
square as shown. Press seam allowances
toward large square.
6. Join a 3" light square to end of each
3-square row as shown. Press seam
allowances toward dark fabric.
7. Join rows to complete block. Press
both joining seams in same direction.
8. Make 50 blocks. Square up blocks to
10½" x 10½".   (Continued)

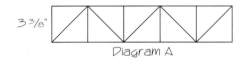

3⅜"

Diagram A

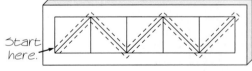

Start
here.

Diagram B

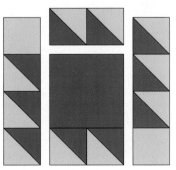

Block Assembly Diagram

MAKING SETTING TRIANGLES

1. Join 1 yellow triangle to 1 side of each gold square (Diagram C). Press seam allowances toward triangle.

2. Join another yellow triangle to adjacent side as shown. Make 20 setting triangles.

JOINING BLOCKS

1. Referring to photo and setting diagrams, lay out blocks and setting triangles in diagonal rows. Move blocks around to achieve balance of color and value.

2. When satisfied with placement, assemble corner units (Diagram D). Sew a setting triangle to opposite sides of corner block; then join corner triangle to top edge as shown. Make 4 corner units.

3. Join 16 blocks for center medallion in 4 rows of 4 blocks each. Join rows to complete medallion square.

4. Measure medallion square through center. Trim 42" border strips to this measurement. Sew 2 borders to opposite edges of medallion square (Diagram E). Press seam allowances toward borders. Join large plaid squares to each end of 2 remaining borders; then join borders to remaining edges of medallion as shown.

5. Working outward from medallion, join blocks in rows (Setting Diagram 1). For Row 1, join 4 blocks and 1 setting triangle; then join row to 1 side of medallion. For Row 2, join 3 blocks and 1 setting triangle; then join row to Row 1. Add corner unit to Row 2 as shown. Turn quilt around and repeat, adding 2 rows and a corner unit to opposite side of quilt.

6. Assemble remaining corners in same manner, joining blocks and setting triangles as shown (Setting Diagram 2).

(Continued)

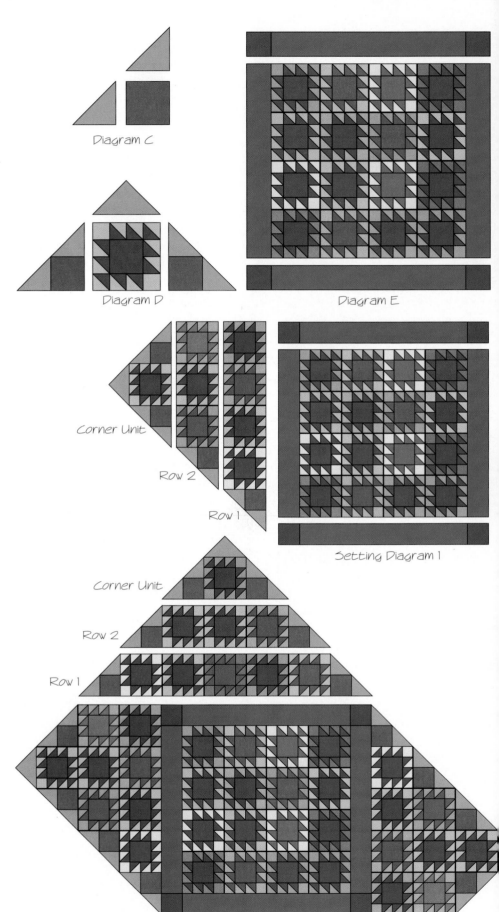

Diagram C

Diagram D

Diagram E

Corner Unit

Row 2

Row 1

Setting Diagram 1

Corner Unit

Row 2

Row 1

Setting Diagram 2

Quilt by Christine N. Brown of Littleton, Colorado

ADDING BORDERS

1. Referring to instructions on page 150, measure quilt; then trim 103" borders to match length and 75" borders to match width.
2. Join long borders to quilt sides. Press seam allowances toward borders.
3. Join large plaid squares to each end of short borders. Sew 1 border strip to top edge of quilt. Repeat for bottom border. Press seam allowances toward borders.

FINISHING

1. Divide backing fabric into 2 (3¼-yard) lengths. Cut 1 piece in half lengthwise. Sew a narrow panel to each side of wide panel. Press seam allowances toward narrow panels.
2. On quilt shown, patchwork is outline-quilted and a small flower is quilted in center of each block (see quilting pattern below). Borders are quilted in a 4"-wide cable design and flower is repeated in corner squares. Mark quilting designs as desired.
3. Layer backing, batting, and quilt top. Baste. Quilt as desired.
4. Make 11 yards of bias or straight-grain binding. See pages 158 and 159 for instructions on making and applying binding.

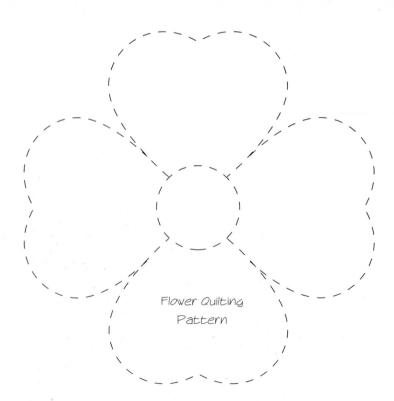

VARIABLE SIZES

Size	Wall/Crib	Twin	King
Finished Size	42" x 42"	66" x 80"	94" x 108"
Number of Blocks	8	25	62
Blocks Set in Medallion	2 x 2	3 x 3	4 x 4
Border Width (finished size)	5" (medallion only)	5"	5"

Flower Quilting Pattern

MIDNIGHT STARS

Like celestial beacons, scraps of bright yellow illuminate this wall hanging's inky sky of medium and dark blue fabrics. The patchwork is easy, but the odd-angled triangles create an illusion of complex piecing.

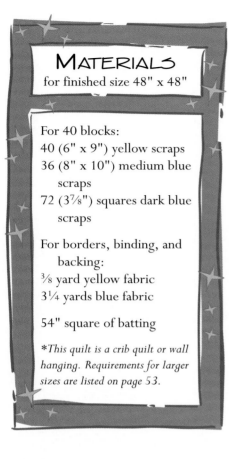

MATERIALS
for finished size 48" x 48"

For 40 blocks:
40 (6" x 9") yellow scraps
36 (8" x 10") medium blue
   scraps
72 (3⅞") squares dark blue
   scraps

For borders, binding, and
   backing:
⅜ yard yellow fabric
3¼ yards blue fabric

54" square of batting

*This quilt is a crib quilt or wall
hanging. Requirements for larger
sizes are listed on page 53.*

CUTTING

Instructions are given for cutting triangles A and B with templates and Triangle C with a rotary cutter and ruler. Make templates for patterns A and B on page 53. Tips on cutting patchwork with templates are on page 144. When marking templates on fabric, mark corners of seam allowances, too.

From *each* yellow scrap, cut:
• 4 of Template B, to get a total of 160 B triangles.

From *each* medium blue scrap, cut:
• 4 of Template A, to get a total of 144 A triangles.

From *each* dark blue square, cut:
• 2 triangles by cutting each square in half diagonally, to get a total of 144 C triangles.

From yellow fabric, cut:
• 4 (2" x 37") strips for inner border.

From blue fabric, cut:
• 2 (27" x 54") lengthwise strips for backing.
• 4 (5" x 37") lengthwise strips for outer border.
• 3 (2½" x 70") lengthwise strips for binding.
• 8 (3⅞") squares. Cut each square in half diagonally to get a total of 16 C triangles for corner blocks.
• 16 of Template A for corner blocks.

MAKING BLOCKS

Finished size of block is 6" square.
1. For 1 block, select 4 each of triangles A and C from assorted scrap fabrics, and 4 Bs of 1 yellow fabric.
2. Matching corner dots and seam allowances carefully, join A and B triangles (Diagram A). Press seam allowances toward blue fabric. Sew A/B unit to C as shown. Press seam allowance toward C. Assembled quarter-block unit should be 3½" square. Make 4 quarter-block units for each block.
3. Join quarter-block units in pairs, turning each unit with yellow B triangle as shown (Block Assembly Diagram). Join pairs to complete block.
4. Make 36 blocks; then make 4 corner blocks in same manner, using A and C triangles of blue border fabric (Corner Block Diagram). Square up blocks to 6½" x 6½".

JOINING BLOCKS

This quilt is an example of a straight set, with 36 blocks set 6 x 6. See setting illustration on page 149. Set aside 4 corner blocks for border.
1. Lay out blocks in 6 horizontal rows of 6 blocks each (Row Assembly Diagram). When satisfied with placement, join blocks in each row.
2. Join rows as shown in photo.

ADDING BORDERS

1. Join each yellow border strip to a blue border strip to make 4 border units. Press seam allowances toward blue borders.
2. Referring to instructions on page 150, measure quilt from top to bottom; then trim 2 border units to match length. Measure quilt from side to side and trim remaining units to match width; then join corner blocks to both ends of these borders.
3. Join first 2 borders to quilt sides. Press seam allowances toward borders. Then join remaining borders to top and bottom edges.

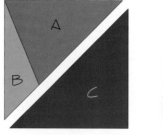

Diagram A

Block Assembly
Diagram

Corner Block
Diagram

Row Assembly Diagram

Quilt by Cynthia Moody Wheeler of Hoover, Alabama

FINISHING

1. Join backing panels to making 54"-square backing. Press seam allowances to 1 side.

2. Mark desired quilting designs on quilt. Quilt shown is outline-quilted.

3. Layer backing, batting, and quilt top. Baste. Quilt as desired.

4. Make 5¾ yards of straight-grain binding. See pages 158 and 159 for instructions on making and applying binding.

5. See page 23 for tips on making a hanging sleeve.

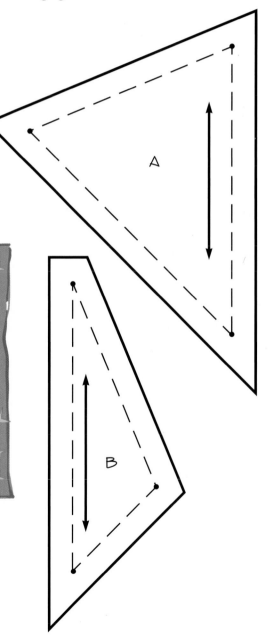

VARIABLE SIZES

Size	Twin	Double/Queen	King
Finished Size	66" x 84"	84" x 90"	96" x 96"
Number of Blocks	112	160	200
Blocks Set	9 x 12	12 x 13	14 x 14
Border Widths (finished size)	1½", 4½"	1½", 4½"	1½", 4½"

NINE-PATCH AND HOURGLASS

An appliquéd vine frames this charming display of alternating blocks. Nine-Patch and Hourglass are two of the basic building blocks of patchwork. See page 59 for instructions on quick-piecing the Hourglass.

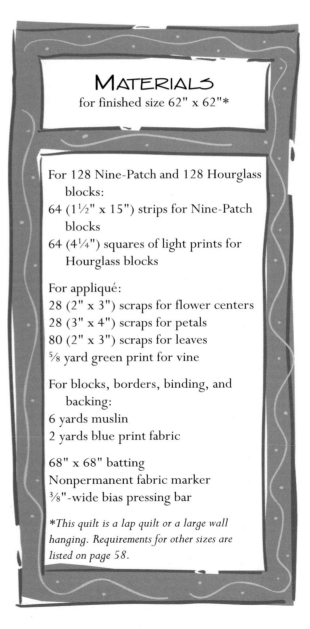

MATERIALS
for finished size 62" x 62"*

For 128 Nine-Patch and 128 Hourglass blocks:
64 (1½" x 15") strips for Nine-Patch blocks
64 (4¼") squares of light prints for Hourglass blocks

For appliqué:
28 (2" x 3") scraps for flower centers
28 (3" x 4") scraps for petals
80 (2" x 3") scraps for leaves
⅝ yard green print for vine

For blocks, borders, binding, and backing:
6 yards muslin
2 yards blue print fabric

68" x 68" batting
Nonpermanent fabric marker
⅜"-wide bias pressing bar

*This quilt is a lap quilt or a large wall hanging. Requirements for other sizes are listed on page 58.

CUTTING

Directions on cutting pieces for hand appliqué are on page 144. Make template for Pattern X on page 58. (*Note:* Same template is used for all flower petals and leaves.) Add seam allowances when cutting fabric.

From muslin, cut:
- 2 (35" x 70") lengthwise strips for backing.
- 4 (5½" x 65") lengthwise strips for middle border.
- 64 (4¼") squares for Hourglass blocks.
- 64 (1½" x 6") strips for Nine-Patch blocks.
- 128 (1½" x 3") strips for Nine-Patch blocks.

From blue fabric, cut:
- 4 (1½" x 66") lengthwise strips for outer border.
- 4 (1½" x 54") lengthwise strips for inner border.
- 1 (28") square for bias binding or 4 (2½" x 66") lengthwise strips for straight-grain binding.
Note: Use leftover blue fabric for patchwork and appliqué, if desired.

From green fabric, cut:
- 1 (21") square for bias appliqué.
Note: Use leftover green fabric for patchwork and appliqué, if desired.

From scraps for appliqué, cut:
- 28 X petals for flower centers.
- 56 X petals for flowers (2 from each fabric).
- 80 X leaves.

MAKING NINE-PATCH BLOCKS

Finished size of block is 3" square.

1. Select 1 (15") scrap strip. Cut strip into 2 (6") lengths and 1 (3") length.

2. Join 6" strips to both sides of 1 (6") muslin strip (Diagram A). Join 2 (3") muslin strips to both sides of 3" scrap. Press seam allowances toward scrap fabric. Then cut each strip set into 1½"-wide segments as shown.

3. Join 3 segments to complete 1 block (Nine-Patch Block Assembly Diagram). You can make 2 blocks from each scrap/muslin combination.

4. Make 128 Nine-Patch blocks. Square up blocks to 3½" x 3½".

Diagram A

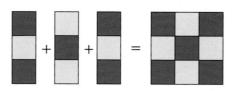

Nine-Patch Block Assembly Diagram

MAKING HOURGLASS BLOCKS

See page 59 for instructions on how to quick-piece Hourglass blocks, using 4¼" squares of scraps and muslin. Make a total of 128 Hourglass blocks. Square up blocks to 3½" x 3½".

JOINING BLOCKS

This quilt is an example of a straight set with alternating blocks. The blocks are set 16 x 16. See setting illustration on page 149.

1. Lay out 16 horizontal rows of 16 blocks each, alternating Nine-Patch and Hourglass blocks (Row Assembly Diagram). Lay out 8 of Row 1, starting with a Nine-Patch, and positioning print triangles of Hourglass blocks adjacent to Nine-Patch blocks. Then lay out 8 of Row 2, starting with an Hourglass block and positioning muslin triangles adjacent to Nine-Patch blocks. When satisfied with placement, join blocks in each row. Press seam allowances toward Hourglass blocks.

2. Join rows.

ADDING BORDERS

1. Read instructions for mitered borders on pages 150 and 151.

2. Measure length of quilt; then mark 2 (54") blue borders to match length. Measure width of quilt and mark 2 borders to match width. Join borders to quilt. Press seam allowances toward borders. Miter corners.

3. In same manner, join muslin borders to quilt and miter corners. Repeat to add blue outer borders. Press seam allowances toward blue borders.

MAKING APPLIQUÉD BORDER

1. See page 158 for tips on making continuous bias. Following those directions, use 21" green square to make 6¾ yards of 1¼"-wide continuous bias. From this, cut 4 (60"-long) strips for appliquéd border.

(Continued)

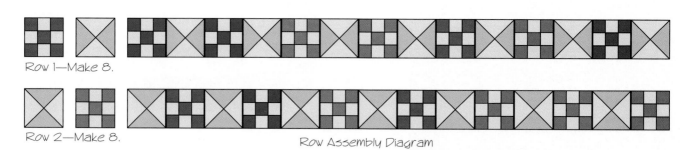

Row 1—Make 8.

Row 2—Make 8.

Row Assembly Diagram

Quilt by Mimi Alef of High Point, North Carolina

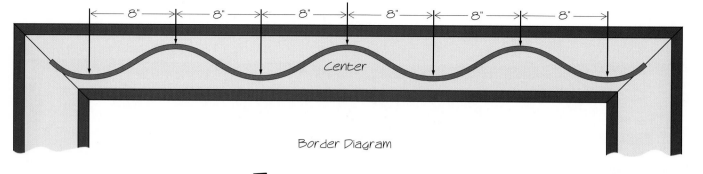

8" | 8" | 8" | 8" | 8" | 8"

Center

Border Diagram

2. See page 69 for tips on bias appliqué. Fold, stitch, and press bias strips as instructed. Prepared vines should be ⅜" wide. Trim seam allowances if necessary.

3. Find center of 1 muslin border strip. Using nonpermanent marker, lightly mark a dot at center point 1" below outer border seam. Alternating from outer seam to inner seam, mark additional placement dots every 8" along length of border strip until you have 7 evenly spaced dots (Border Diagram). Each dot should be 1" from seam. Repeat for all muslin border strips.

4. Fold 1 bias strip in half to find center. Pin center of vine at center dot on border. Working out from center, pin vine in place, curving bias up and down from dot to dot as shown. Pin ends of vine at mitered seam. In same manner, pin vines on remaining muslin border strips. Don't worry if vines don't meet precisely at corners, since ends will be covered by a leaf. When satisfied with position of vines, appliqué.

5. Prepare petals and leaves for appliqué. Directions on preparing pieces for hand appliqué are on page 147.

6. Select 2 matching petals and 1 center for each flower. Referring to photo on page 57, position a flower in each curve of vine. Appliqué flower center first; then overlap petals as shown on pattern and appliqué. Stitch 28 flowers in place around border as shown.

7. Appliqué a leaf at each corner, aligning it with mitered seam. Add a second leaf near each corner as shown. Place remaining leaves on vine in groups of 3 as shown and appliqué.

FINISHING

1. Join 2 strips of backing fabric lengthwise. Press seam allowances to 1 side.

2. On quilt shown, patchwork and appliqué are outline-quilted. Mark quilting designs as desired.

3. Layer backing, batting, and quilt top. Baste. Quilt as desired.

4. Make 7¼ yards of bias or straight-grain binding. See pages 158 and 159 for instructions on making and applying binding.

5. See page 23 for tips on making a hanging sleeve.

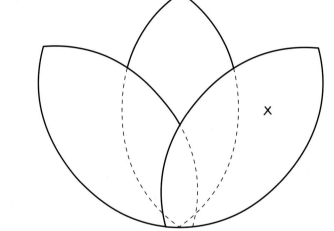

Border Flower Appliqué Pattern and Placement Guide

VARIABLE SIZES

Size	Twin	Double/Queen	King
Finished Size	62" x 86"	88" x 97"	97" x 97"
Number of Nine-Patch Blocks	192	336	392
Number of Hourglass Blocks	192	336	392
Blocks Set	16 x 24	24 x 28	28 x 28
Border Widths (finished size)	1", 5", 1"	1", 5", 1"	1", 5", 1"

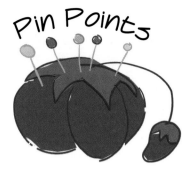

QUICK-PIECED HOURGLASS BLOCKS

Here's an easy method for making Hourglass blocks in minutes! When making several Hourglass blocks from the same two-fabric combination, it's faster and more accurate to quick-piece the blocks than to cut and sew individual triangles.

1. For our *Nine-Patch and Hourglass*, use 4¼" squares of muslin and print fabrics to make Hourglass blocks (finished size 3"). This technique requires a square of each fabric that is 1¼" larger than the desired *finished* size of the block. You will get two Hourglass blocks from each set of matching squares.

2. On the wrong side of each muslin square, draw diagonal lines from corner to corner in *both* directions. With right sides facing, match one marked square with one square of scrap fabric.

3. Stitch a ¼" seam on *both* sides of one diagonal line (Diagram A). Press stitching.

4. Cut units apart on the line between stitching (Diagram B). Press units open, pressing the seam allowance toward the scrap fabric. You will have two triangle-squares (Diagram C).

5. On the wrong side of one triangle-square, extend the drawn line from the corner of the muslin triangle to the corner of the scrap triangle. Then match both triangle-squares with contrasting fabrics facing and the marked unit on top.

6. Stitch a ¼" seam on *both* sides of the marked line (Diagram D).

7. Cut the units apart between the stitching line as before (Diagram E). Press both units open to get two Hourglass blocks (Diagram F). In our example, the blocks will measure 3½" square (including seam allowances). When joined, the finished size of the blocks will be 3" square.

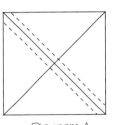
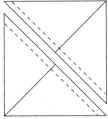

Diagram A   Diagram B

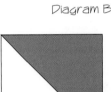

Diagram C

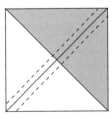

Diagram D   Diagram E

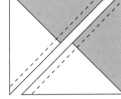

Diagram F

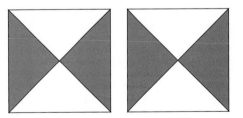

A Piece of Cake

A luscious print adds elegance to scrap blocks.
These Cake Stand blocks, pieced in the colors of spring,
are surrounded by setting pieces of flowery pink and mint fabrics.
Use leftovers to make a prairie point edging.

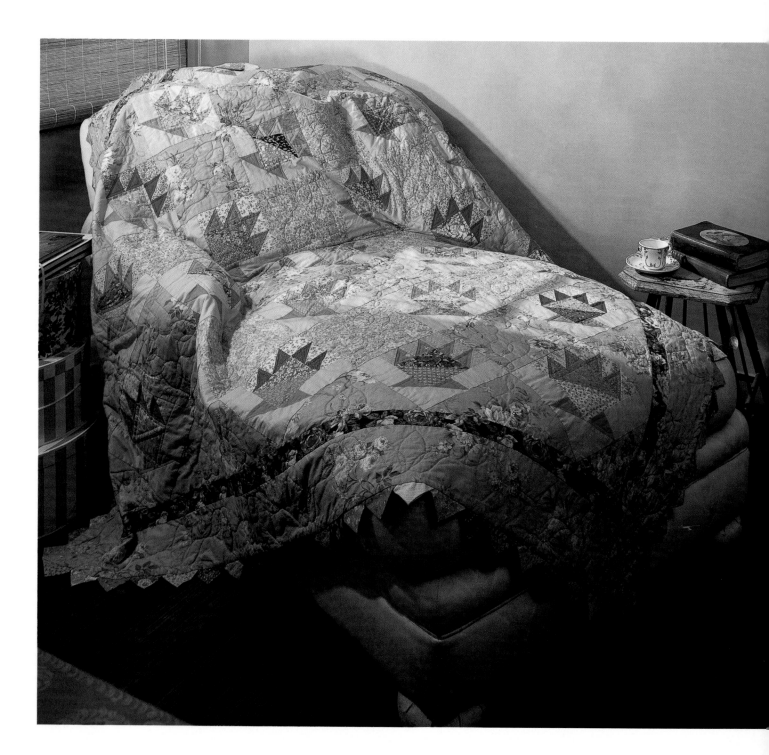

MATERIALS

for finished size 69" x 91"*

For 35 blocks:
70 (7") squares pastel scraps
35 (4⅞") squares pastel
     scraps
1⅛ yards pink solid fabric
⅜ yard rose solid fabric

For setting pieces and
     borders:
3 yards mint print fabric
¾ yard pink print fabric
½ yard dark green print
     fabric

5½ yards backing fabric or
     2¾ yards 90"-wide muslin
81" x 96" precut batting

*This quilt fits a twin bed.
Requirements for other sizes are
listed on page 62.

CUTTING

Cut all strips cross-grain unless stated
otherwise.

From each of 35 (7") squares, cut:
• 1 (3¾") square for prairie points.
• 2 (2⅞") squares. Cut each square in
  half diagonally to get 4 B triangles.
• 1 (2½") A square.

**From each of remaining 35 (7")
squares, cut:**
• 2 (3¾") squares for prairie points.
• 2 (2⅞") squares. Cut each square in
  half diagonally to get 4 B triangles.

From each 4⅞" square, cut:
• 2 C triangles by cutting each square in
  half diagonally, to get a total of 70 C
  triangles.

From pink solid fabric, cut:
• 8 (2½"-wide) strips. From these, cut
  70 (2½" x 4½") D strips.
• 18 (4⅞") squares. Cut each square in
  half diagonally to get 35 C triangles
  and 1 extra.

From rose solid fabric, cut:
• 5 (3¾") squares for prairie points.
• 35 (2⅞") squares. Cut each square in
  half diagonally to get 70 B triangles.

From mint print fabric, cut:
• 2 (5" x 96") lengthwise strips and 2
  (5" x 76") lengthwise strips for outer
  border.
• 5 (12⅝") squares. Cut each square in
  quarters diagonally to get 20 setting
  triangles.
• 12 (8½") setting squares.
• 2 (6½") squares. Cut each square in
  half diagonally to get 4 corner
  triangles.

From pink print fabric, cut:
• 12 (8½") setting squares.
• 12 (3¾") squares for prairie points.

From dark green print fabric, cut:
• 8 (2"-wide) strips for inner border.

MAKING BLOCKS

Finished size of block is 8" square.
1. For "cake" portion of each block,
select 1 A square and 4 B triangles of 1
pastel fabric, 4 B triangles of a second
pastel fabric, and 2 C triangles.

2. Join B triangles in pairs to make 4
triangle-squares. Join C triangles in
same manner. Press seam allowances
toward darker fabric.
3. Join B triangle-squares in pairs as
shown (Diagram A). Join 1 pair to top
edge of C triangle-square. Press seam
allowances toward C.
4. Join A square to 1 end of remaining
pair as shown. Press seam allowance
toward A. Join 3-square unit to side of C
triangle-square as shown.
5. Join 2 rose B triangles to ends of 2
D rectangles. Join units to sides of cake
unit (Block Assembly Diagram). Press
seam allowances toward Ds. Join pink C
triangle to corner to complete block.
6. Make 35 blocks. Square up blocks to
8½" x 8½".   (Continued)

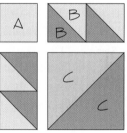

Diagram A

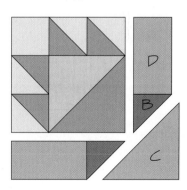

Block Assembly Diagram

JOINING BLOCKS

This quilt is an example of a diagonal set with alternating blocks. The blocks are set 5 x 7.

1. Lay out blocks and setting pieces in 11 diagonal rows (Quilt Assembly Diagram). Pay careful attention to placement of pink and mint setting squares. Move blocks around to achieve balance of color and value.

2. When satisfied with placement, join blocks in each row. Press seam allowances toward setting pieces. Referring to photo, join rows.

ADDING BORDERS

1. Read instructions for mitered borders on pages 150 and 151.

2. Join 2 dark green border strips for each side of quilt. Matching centers, join 1 dark green border strip to each mint border. Trim ends of dark green border to match each mint border.

3. Measure length of quilt; then mark 2 longer border units to match length. Measure width of quilt and mark 2 remaining borders to match width. Join borders to quilt. Press seam allowances toward borders. Miter corners.

FINISHING

1. Divide backing fabric into 2 (2¾-yard) lengths. Cut 1 piece in half lengthwise. Sew a narrow panel to each side of wide panel. Press seam allowances toward narrow panels.

2. Mark desired quilting designs on quilt top. The quilt shown has flowers and hearts quilted in setting squares and triangles. Select a cable or other suitable design for borders.

3. Layer backing, batting, and quilt top. Baste. Quilt as desired. Quilting should not come closer than ½" from edge of quilt. Do not trim batting and backing yet.

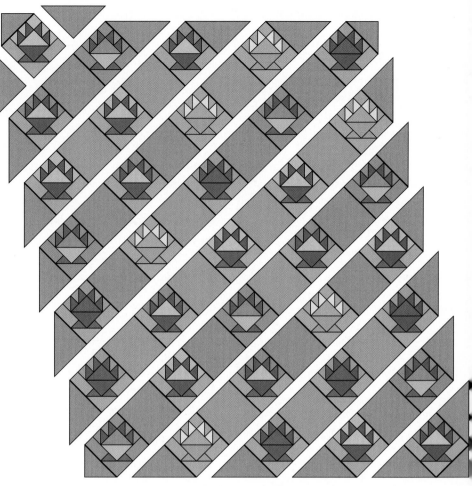

Quilt Assembly Diagram

VARIABLE SIZES

Size	Wall/Crib	Double/Queen	King
Finished Size	46" x 46"	80½" x 91"	91" x 91"
Number of Blocks	9	42	49
Blocks Set	3 x 3	6 x 7	7 x 7
Setting Squares Pink Green	none 4	14 16	16 20
Setting Triangles	8	22	24
Border Widths (finished size)	1½", 4½"	1½", 4½"	1½", 4½"

4. To make prairie points, fold 3¾" squares in half (Diagram B); then fold each piece in half again to make a small triangle (Diagram C).

5. On right side of quilt, arrange 35 prairie points along each side, with each triangle overlapping its neighbor as needed to fit (Diagram D). Aligning raw edges of triangles and quilt border, space prairie points evenly and baste through top and batting only, keeping backing free. Position and baste 26 prairie points each at top and bottom edges.

6. Folding backing out of the way, stitch prairie points in place through top and batting (Diagram E).

7. Trim batting even with quilt top. Trim backing 1" larger on all sides. Turn under raw edge of backing, covering raw edges of prairie points, and blindstitch backing in place (Diagram F).

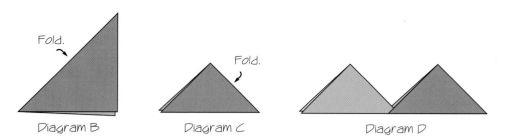

Diagram B   Diagram C   Diagram D

Diagram E

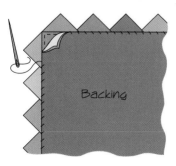

Diagram F

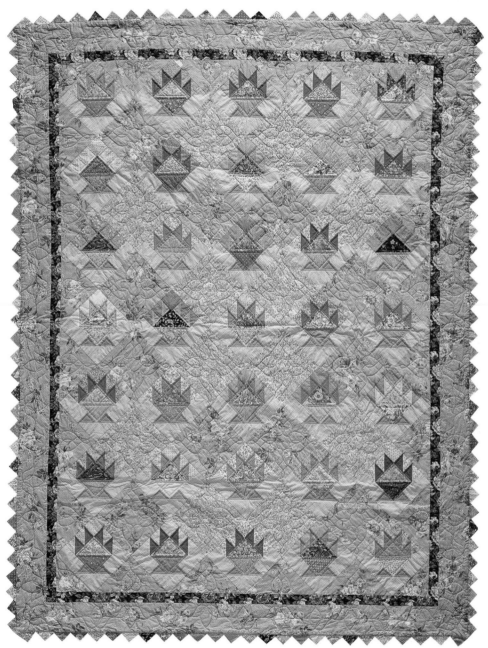

Quilt by Beth Meek of Windham, New Hampshire, from a design by Donna Lucidi of Ephrata, Pennsylvania

CROSSED TULIPS

To create the illusion of a continuous,
undulating vine, the blocks are joined in double rows
before the bias appliqué is completed.

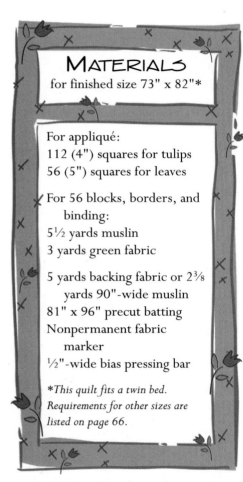

MATERIALS
for finished size 73" x 82"*

For appliqué:
112 (4") squares for tulips
56 (5") squares for leaves

For 56 blocks, borders, and
    binding:
5½ yards muslin
3 yards green fabric

5 yards backing fabric or 2⅜
    yards 90"-wide muslin
81" x 96" precut batting
Nonpermanent fabric
    marker
½"-wide bias pressing bar

*This quilt fits a twin bed.
Requirements for other sizes are
listed on page 66.

CUTTING

Directions on cutting pieces for hand appliqué are on page 144. Make templates for patterns A and B on page 68. Add seam allowances when cutting fabric.

Cut all strips cross-grain unless stated otherwise.

From 4" squares, cut:
• 112 A tulips.

From 5" squares, cut:
• 112 B leaves.

From muslin, cut:
• 2 (4½" x 87") lengthwise strips and 2 (4½" x 78") lengthwise strips for border.
• 56 (9¼") squares.

From green fabric, cut:
• 1 (30") square for bias binding or 8 (2½"-wide) strips for straight-grain binding.
• 2 (35") squares for bias appliqué. *Note:* Use leftover green fabric for leaves, if desired.

MAKING BLOCKS

Finished size of block is 9¼" square.
1. For each block, select 1 muslin square, 2 A tulips, and 2 B leaves. Prepare tulips and leaves for appliqué. Directions on preparing pieces for hand appliqué are on page 147.
2. Fold each square in half vertically, horizontally, and diagonally in both directions, finger-pressing creases for placement guides.

3. Place muslin square over pattern, matching placement guides with fold lines on pattern. Lightly trace 1 tulip, stem, and 1 leaf onto half of muslin. Then turn muslin upside down, aligning placement lines, and trace again for other half.
4. See page 158 for tips on making continuous bias. Following those directions, use 35" green squares to make 38 yards of 1½"-wide continuous bias. From this, cut 42 (24"-long) strips and 28 (12"-long) strips for appliquéd stems.
5. See page 69 for tips on bias appliqué. Fold, stitch, and press bias strips as instructed. Prepared stems should be ½" wide.
6. On each muslin square, position 2 B leaves and appliqué.
7. On 1 block, position 1 (12"-long) stem, letting end of strip extend at edge of block. Appliqué sides of strip to muslin, stitching inside curve first and then outside curve. Place 1 A tulip over top of stem and appliqué. Sew second tulip in place, leaving 1" unstitched at bottom of tulip so stem can be inserted later. Repeat to make a total of 26 blocks for outside edges of quilt.
8. On remaining 30 blocks, appliqué leaves and tulips in place, leaving space in tulips to insert stems later.

(Continued)

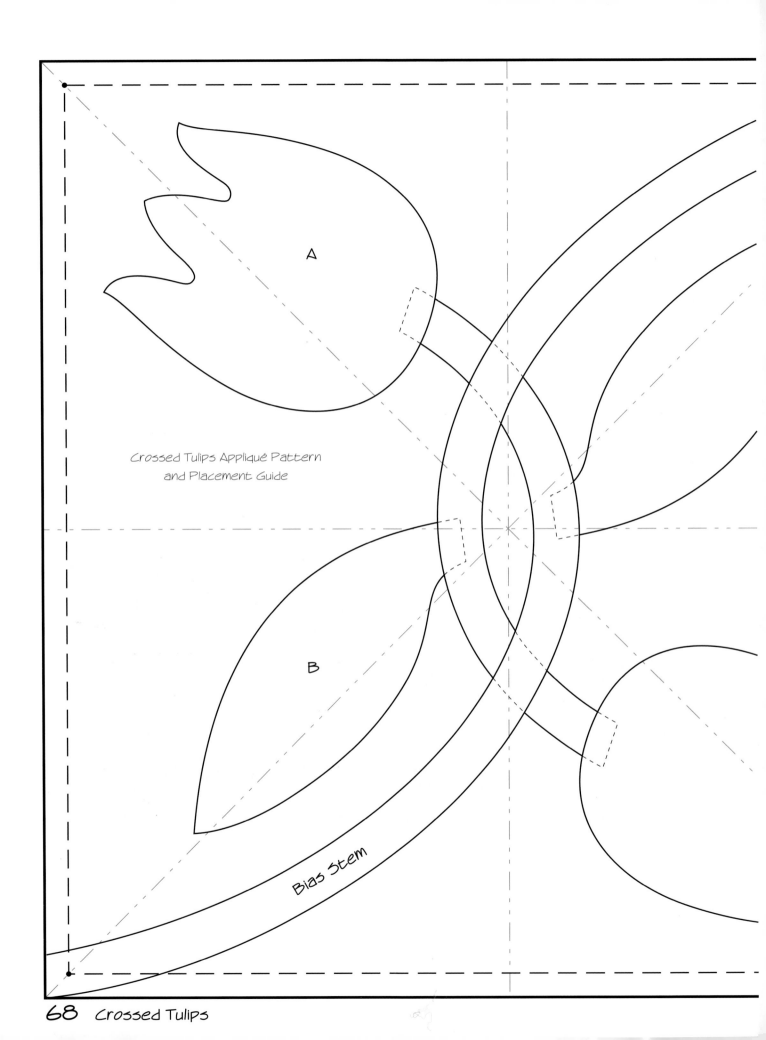

Crossed Tulips Appliqué Pattern
and Placement Guide

A

B

Bias Stem

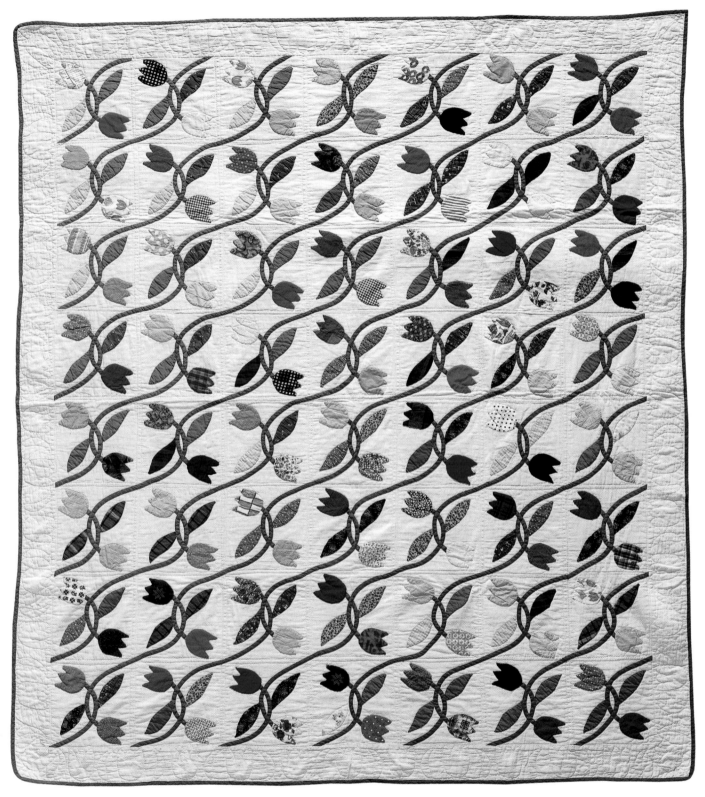

Antique quilt owned by Carolyn B. Maruggi of Pittsford, New York

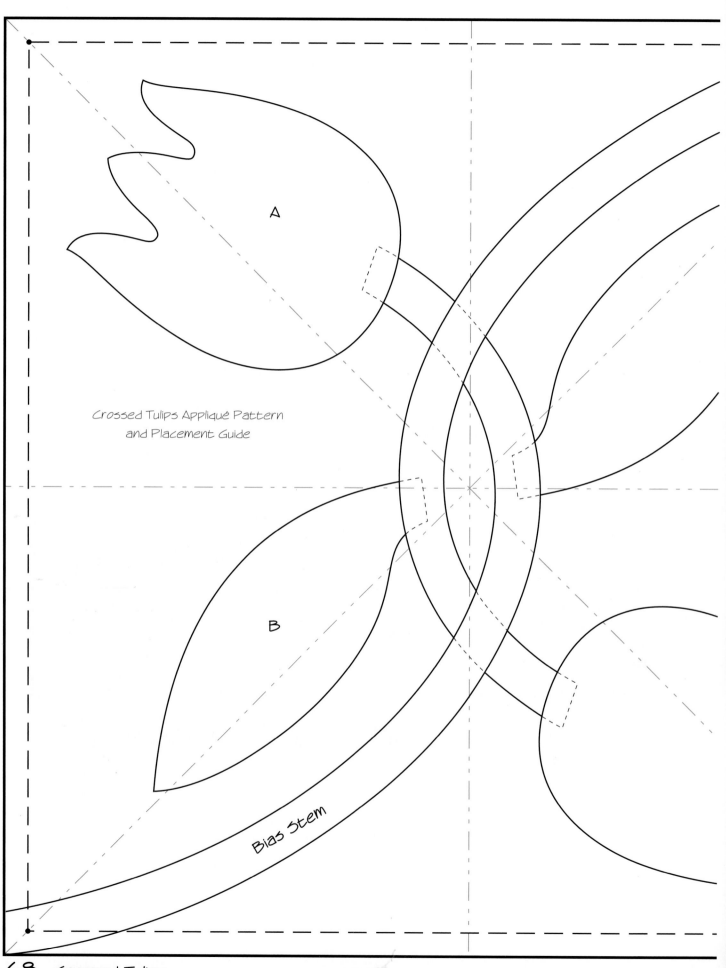

Crossed Tulips Appliqué Pattern
and Placement Guide

A

B

Bias Stem

JOINING BLOCKS

This quilt is an example of a straight set, with the blocks set 7 x 8. See setting illustration on page 149.

1. Lay out blocks in 8 horizontal rows, with 7 blocks in each row (Row Assembly Diagram). Referring to photo, place blocks with 1 stem appliqué at outside edges. When satisfied with placement, join blocks in each row. Press seam allowances in opposite directions from row to row.

2. Appliqué 1 remaining 12"-long stem onto blocks at top left corner and bottom right corner of your layout. Stitch bottom of tulip over end of stem.

3. Join first and second rows as shown. Before adding third row, position 6 (24"-long) stems (indicated by broken lines) and appliqué. When appliqué is complete, add third row and add stems as before. Continue adding rows and appliquéing stems until all rows are joined and stems are in place.

ADDING BORDERS

1. Read instructions for mitered borders on pages 150 and 151.

2. Measure length of quilt; then mark 2 longer border strips to match length. Measure width of quilt and mark 2 remaining borders to match width. Join borders to quilt. Press seam allowances toward borders. Miter corners.

FINISHING

1. Divide backing fabric into 2 (2½-yard) lengths. Cut 1 piece in half lengthwise. Sew a narrow panel to each side of wide panel. Press seam allowances toward narrow panels.

2. Select a cable or other suitable design for border. Mark border design on quilt top.

3. Layer backing, batting, and quilt top. Baste. Outline-quilt appliqué; then quilt borders as desired.

4. Make 9 yards of bias or straight-grain binding. See pages 158 and 159 for instructions on making and applying binding.

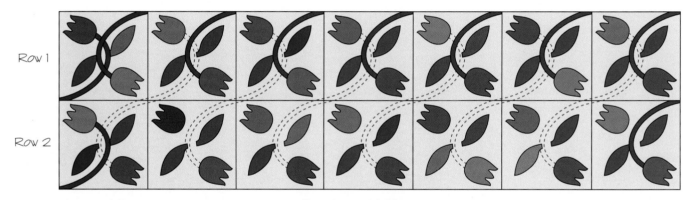

Row 1

Row 2

Row Assembly Diagram

VARIABLE SIZES

Size	Wall/Crib	Double/Queen	King
Finished Size	45" x 54"	88" x 97"	101" x 101"
Number of Blocks	20	72	81
Blocks Set	4 x 5	8 x 9	9 x 9
Border Width (finished size)	4"	6"	8"

CRACKER

The tiniest scraps can be useful in making this block,
reminiscent of popping party favors. A consistent
neutral fabric, in this case a mottled tan, brings
order to the profusion of color and prints.

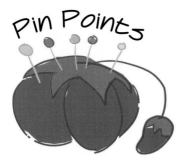

Pin Points

BIAS APPLIQUÉ

The flower stems in *Crossed Tulips* (page 64) are made with bias strips. This same technique for making curved stems is also used to make undulating vines in the border of *Nine-Patch and Hourglass* (page 54).

Use *bias pressing bars*, made of metal or heat-resistant plastic, to prepare bias for appliqué. Available in sets of varying widths, bias bars are sold at quilt shops and through mail-order catalogs.

Start with a square of fabric. Instructions state the size square required and the width of the bias strips to be cut.

1. Cut bias strips as described in the project instructions. With wrong sides facing and edges aligned, fold one strip in half lengthwise. Machine-stitch a scant ¼" from the edges, making a narrow tube. Slide the tube over the pressing bar, centering the seam on the flat side of the bar. Press seam allowances to one side or open, as you prefer. (Be careful when handling metal bars—they get hot!) Remove the bar. Trim seam allowances as necessary.

2. With the seam against the background fabric, baste or pin a bias strip in place over the traced appliqué guide lines. A steam iron will help shape the strip as desired. Appliqué the sides of the strip onto the background fabric, stitching the inside curves first and then the outside curves so that the bias will lie flat.

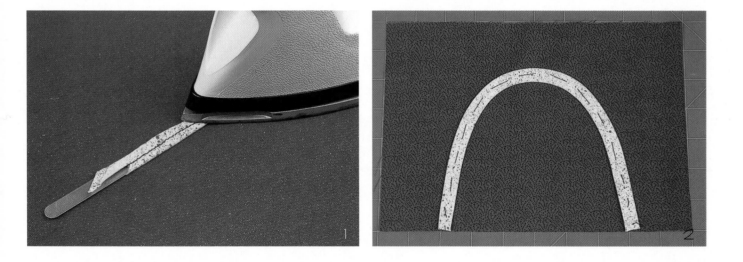

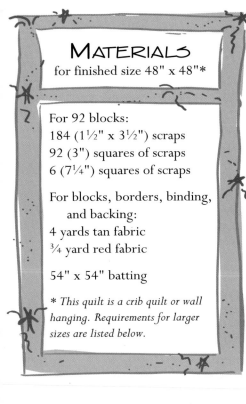

MATERIALS
for finished size 48" x 48"*

For 92 blocks:
184 (1½" x 3½") scraps
92 (3") squares of scraps
6 (7¼") squares of scraps

For blocks, borders, binding, and backing:
4 yards tan fabric
¾ yard red fabric

54" x 54" batting

This quilt is a crib quilt or wall hanging. Requirements for larger sizes are listed below.

CUTTING
Cut all strips cross-grain unless stated otherwise.

From *each* 3" square, cut:
• 2 triangles by cutting each square in half diagonally to get a total of 184 triangles for blocks.

From *each* 7¼" square, cut:
• 4 triangles by cutting each square in quarters diagonally to get a total of 24 triangles for border.

From tan fabric, cut:
• 2 (30" x 58") lengthwise strips for backing.
• 4 (1½" x 38") lengthwise strips for inner border.
• 92 (1½" x 3½") strips for blocks.
• 92 (3") squares. Cut each square in half diagonally to get a total of 184 triangles.
• 6 (7¼") squares. Cut each square in quarters diagonally to get a total of 24 triangles for border.

From red fabric, cut:
• 1 (24") square for bias binding or 5 (2½"-wide) strips for straight-grain binding.

MAKING BLOCKS
Finished size of block is 4¼" square.

1. For each block, select 2 small tan triangles, 2 small scrap triangles, 2 (1½" x 3½") scrap strips and 1 same-size tan strip.

2. Join scrap strips to both sides of tan strip (*Block Assembly Diagram*). Press seam allowances toward scraps. Joined strips should measure 3½" square.

3. Join tan triangles to scrap side of square as shown. Press seam allowances toward scraps. Then join scrap triangles to top and bottom edges as shown to complete block. Press seam allowances toward scrap triangles.

4. Make 92 blocks. Square up blocks to 4¾" x 4¾".

Block Assembly Diagram

VARIABLE SIZES

Size	Twin	Double/Queen	King
Finished Size	66" x 86"	86" x 99"	99" x 99"
Number of Interior Blocks	204	340	400
Blocks Set	12 x 17	17 x 20	20 x 20
Inner Border Width (finished size)	1½"	2"	2"
Number of Border Blocks	48	60	64
Border Blocks Set	10 x 14	14 x 16	16 x 16

JOINING BLOCKS

This quilt is an example of a straight set, with 64 blocks set 8 x 8. See setting illustration on page 149. Set aside remaining 28 blocks for border.

1. Lay out blocks in 8 horizontal rows of 8 blocks each (Row Assembly Diagram). Lay out 4 of Row 1, with first block's scrap triangles tipped to the right, and alternate left and right directions across row. Then lay out 4 of Row 2, starting with a block tipped to the left. When satisfied with placement, join blocks in each row.

2. Join rows, alternating rows 1 and 2 as shown in photo

ADDING BORDERS

1. For each border, select 7 blocks and 6 each of tan and scrap large triangles.

2. Lay out blocks in a row (Border Assembly Diagram). Positioning blocks as shown, sew a tan triangle to 1 side of first 6 blocks. Set aside first block; then sew a scrap triangle to opposite edge of remaining blocks. Press seam allowances toward triangles.

3. Join blocks in row as shown. Make 4 border rows.

4. Matching centers, join tan inner border strip to top edge (tan triangles) of each pieced border. Press seam allowances toward inner border.

5. Read instructions for mitered borders on pages 150 and 151. Measure length of quilt; then mark 2 inner border strips to match length. Measure width of quilt and mark 2 remaining borders to match width. Join borders to quilt, easing as necessary. Press seam allowances toward borders. Miter corners.

FINISHING

1. Join 2 strips of backing fabric lengthwise. Press seam allowances to 1 side.

2. On quilt shown, patchwork is outline-quilted. Patterns are below for small quatrefoil quilted in tan triangles where 4 blocks come together and for cluster of feathers quilted in tan border triangles extending into inner border. Mark quilting designs as desired.

3. Layer backing, batting, and quilt top. Baste. Quilt as desired.

4. Make 5¾ yards of bias or straight-grain binding. See pages 158 and 159 for instructions on making and applying binding.

5. See page 23 for tips on making a hanging sleeve.

Row 1—Make 4.

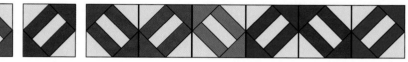

Row 2—Make 4.

Row Assembly Diagram

Border Assembly Diagram

Block Quilting Pattern

Border Quilting Pattern

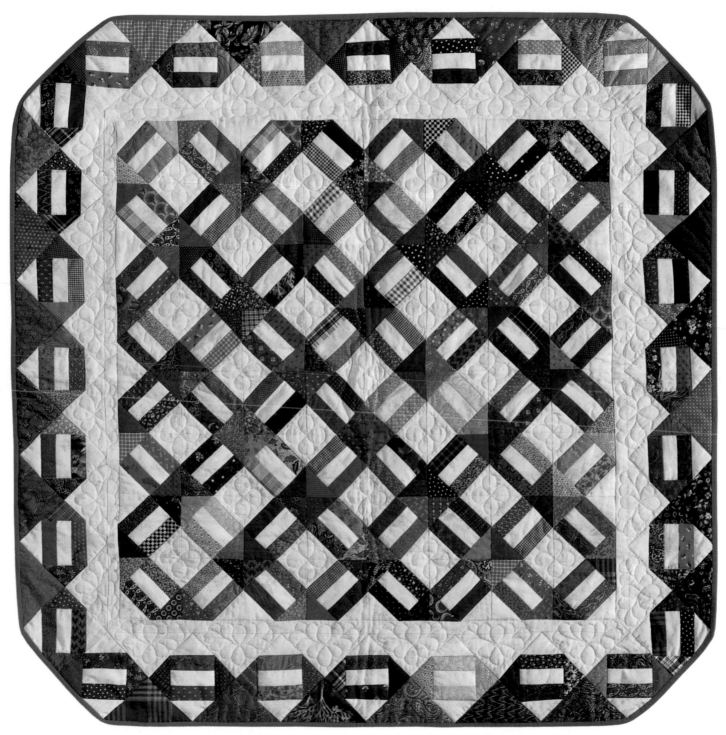

Quilt by Mimi Alef of High Point, North Carolina

STARRY NIGHT

This quilt captures the image of dawn, with
scraps of progressively darker
blues surrounding stars that fade
into the new day.
Because of the random
placement of stars, this quilt
is assembled in horizontal sections

MATERIALS

for finished size 74" x 86"*

86 (3½") squares light blue scraps
99 (3½") squares medium blue
    scraps
151 (3½") squares dark blue
    scraps
9 (3⅞") squares light blue scraps
10 (3⅞") squares medium blue
    scraps
24 (3⅞") squares dark blue scraps
2⅜ yards muslin
2⅝ yards striped fabric for
    borders
⅞ yard navy solid for binding

5½ yards backing fabric or
    2¾ yards 90"-wide muslin
81" x 96" precut batting

*This quilt fits a twin bed. Adapting this
design for other sizes is not recommended.*

CUTTING

From *each* 3⅞" square, cut:

- 2 triangles by cutting each square in half diagonally, to get a total of 86 triangles for star points.

From muslin, cut:

- 11 (6½") squares for star centers.
- 35 (5¼") squares.
  Cut each square in quarters diagonally to get 4 triangles, for a total of 140 triangles for border.
- 43 (3⅞") squares.
  Cut each square in half diagonally to get 2 triangles, for a total of 86 triangles for star points.

From striped fabric, cut:

- 2 (3½" x 64") lengthwise strips and 2 (3½" x 76") lengthwise strips for inner border.
- 2 (3½" x 78") lengthwise strips and 2 (3½" x 90") lengthwise strips for outer border.

From navy fabric, cut:

- 1 (31") square for bias binding or 8 (2½" x 42") strips for straight-grain binding.

QUILT TOP ASSEMBLY

The success of this quilt depends on artfully arranging light, medium, and dark scraps by value to create an image of night and day.

This quilt is assembled in 8 horizontal sections. Lay out all the pieces on the floor, a large table, or a felt-covered design wall before beginning to sew. Study the photo on page 79 carefully as you lay out each section.

1. Set aside 70 (3½") squares for pieced border, choosing 24 light, 22 medium, and 24 dark fabrics.

2. Starting with lightest scraps, lay out pieces for Section 1 (Quilt Assembly Diagram). Arrange squares and triangles in 18 vertical rows of 4 squares each, combining 2 rows to accommodate star centers as shown. Lay out remaining sections in same manner. Rearrange pieces until satisfied with placement.

3. Join each pair of blue and muslin triangles to make star points. Press seam allowances toward blue fabric. Trim each triangle-square to 3½" square and return it to layout.

4. Starting with Section 1, pick up first vertical row of squares and join as shown; then return row to layout. Join second vertical row in same manner. For rows 3 and 4, join squares in each row; then join rows and sew double row to top of star square. Join remaining rows in same manner.

5. In every other row, press seam allowances toward top square. In alternate rows, press seam allowances toward bottom square. Treat double rows as 1 row for pressing.

6. Join rows from left to right to complete Section 1.

7. Assemble sections 2–8 in same manner, checking assembled rows against diagram as you work.

8. Join assembled sections to complete main part of quilt. (Continued)

Pin Points

METRIC EQUIVALENTS

For our quilting friends in other lands, here's a helpful hint for converting inches and yards to centimeters and meters.

- Multiply inches and fractions of inches by 2.54 to find centimeters. For example, ¼" equals .64 cm (.25" x 2.54 = .635 cm) and 3½" equals 8.9 cm (3.5" x 2.54 = 8.89 cm).
- Multiply yards and fractions of yards by .9 to find meters. For example, 4⅜ yards equals 3.94 meters (4.375 yards x .9 = 3.938 m).

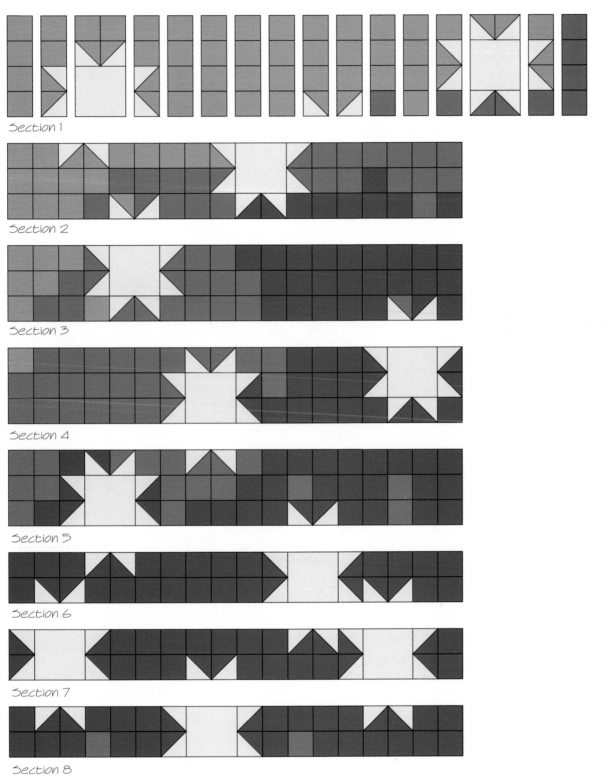

Section 1

Section 2

Section 3

Section 4

Section 5

Section 6

Section 7

Section 8

Quilt Assembly Diagram

Adding Borders

1. Read instructions for mitered borders on pages 150 and 151. Measure length of quilt; then mark 2 (76"-long) inner border strips to match length. Measure width of quilt and mark 2 (64"-long) borders to match width. Join borders to quilt, easing as necessary. Press seam allowances toward borders. Miter corners.

2. Trim 70 remaining blue squares to 3⅜" square before piecing border.

3. For top border, select 16 light and medium blue squares and 32 muslin triangles. Referring to photo, lay out pieces in a row. Starting at left corner, sew a triangle to 2 adjacent sides of first square (Border Assembly Diagram). For remaining squares in row, sew triangles to opposite edges as shown. Press seam allowances toward squares. Join units in a row as shown. Using 16 dark blue squares, assemble bottom border in same manner.

4. Matching centers, join pieced borders to top and bottom edges of quilt. Press seam allowances toward inner border.

5. Use 19 squares and 38 triangles to assemble each side border. Matching centers, join borders to quilt sides, easing as necessary. Miter border corners.

6. Measuring quilt as before, join striped outer borders to quilt and miter corners.

Finishing

1. Divide backing fabric into 2 (2¾-yard) lengths. Cut 1 piece in half lengthwise. Sew a narrow panel to each side of wide panel. Press seam allowances toward narrow panels.

2. Layer backing, batting, and quilt top. Baste. Quilt as desired. On quilt shown, free-style swirls are quilted over the patchwork and borders are outline-quilted.

3. Make 9¼ yards of bias or straight-grain binding. See pages 158 and 159 for instructions on making and applying binding.

4. See page 23 for tips on making a hanging sleeve, if desired.

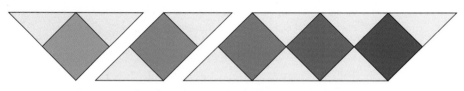

Border Assembly Diagram

Pin Points

Mail-Order Resources

Quiltmaking supplies are available at many craft and fabric stores, especially quilting specialty shops. Consult your telephone directory to find a shop in your area.

If you prefer to have things delivered to your door, you can order supplies from a mail-order source. The following catalogs are excellent suppliers of fabric, notions, and miscellaneous quilting supplies. Both companies have toll-free telephone numbers and will mail you a catalog at no charge.

Keepsake Quilting
P.O. Box 1618
Centre Harbor, NH 03226
(800) 865-9458

Connecting Threads
5750 N.E. Hassalo
Portland, OR 97213
(800) 574-6454

Quilt by Beverly Leasure of Dunedin, Florida

HEXAGON PUZZLE

The stars in this quilt look intricate, but they're easier
to sew than you might think. Pieced hexagons combine with triangles
to make the stars shine. And it's all sewn in straight
lines by making vertical rows instead of blocks.

MATERIALS
for finished size 63" x 72"*

For 35 stars and binding:
35 (9" x 18") scraps

For background and borders:
4 yards muslin

4 yards backing fabric
72" x 90" precut batting

*This quilt fits a twin bed. Require-
ments for other sizes are below.

CUTTING

Make templates for patterns A, B, and C
on page 83. Refer to page 144 for tips
on making templates.

From *each* scrap fabric, cut:
• 1 (2½" x 9") strip for binding.
• 6 *each* of templates A and B.

From muslin, cut:
• 4 (5" x 66") lengthwise strips for
  border.
• 98 of Template B.
• 115 of Template C.

QUILT TOP ASSEMBLY

Because this quilt is assembled in vertical
rows, you won't see the stars until rows
are joined.

1. For each star, select 6 A diamonds
and 6 B triangles of matching fabrics.

2. Join 3 A diamonds in a row to make
2 half-hexagons (Diagram A). Join 2
halves to complete hexagon. Press all
seam allowances in same direction.

3. Positioning hexagon as shown
(Diagram B), join matching B triangles to
opposite edges. Press seam allowances
toward triangles. Make 35 of these
diamond-shaped star units.

(Continued)

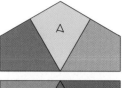

Diagram A

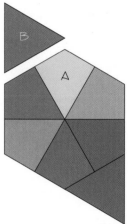

Diagram B

VARIABLE SIZES

Size	Wall/Crib	Double/Queen	King
Finished Size	40½" x 56"	85" x 88"	94" x 103"
Number of Stars	7	71	97
Number of Vertical Rows	13	17	19
Border Width (finished size)	4½"	4½"	4½"

4. For Row 1, lay out 20 muslin B triangles, 4 scrap B triangles, and 13 muslin C hexagons in a vertical row (Row Assembly Diagram). For Row 2, lay out 7 muslin Bs, 11 scrap Bs, 8 muslin Cs, and 4 star units. Match scrap triangles to fabrics in adjacent star units as shown. For Row 3, lay out 4 muslin Bs, 14 scrap Bs, 10 muslin Cs, and 3 star units.

5. Continue laying out rows, alternating rows 2 and 3 (see photo), until you have 5 each of rows 2 and 3. For last row (Row 4), lay out 23 muslin B triangles, 3 scrap B triangles, and 12 muslin C hexagons. Move pieced units around until satisfied with placement and color balance.

6. In each row, join triangles to hexagons to create diamond-shaped units as shown. Return each completed unit to row layout to confirm placement before you continue. Then join units to complete each row.

7. When all rows are complete and you are satisfied with placement, join rows. Pin adjacent rows together and check to be sure scrap triangles and star units align correctly before you stitch.

8. When all rows are joined, trim excess from pieces at top and bottom of each row as shown in diagram. Align a ruler with seam allowances at top of each row 2 and rotary-cut through muslin Bs and Cs to remove extra fabric. Repeat across top of quilt as needed to trim all rows. Trim bottom edge of quilt in same manner.

Row Assembly Diagram

Quilt by Betty Lou Wilder of West Orange, New Jersey

ADDING BORDERS

1. Referring to instructions on page 150, measure quilt from top to bottom; then trim 2 border strips to match length. Join borders to quilt sides. Press seam allowances toward borders.

2. Measure quilt from side to side; then trim remaining borders to match quilt width. Join borders to top and bottom edges. Press seam allowances toward borders.

FINISHING

1. Divide backing fabric into 2 (2-yard) lengths. Cut 1 piece in half lengthwise. Sew a narrow panel to each side of wide panel. Press seam allowances toward narrow panels.

2. On quilt shown, star pieces are quilted in-the-ditch and a flower-like feathered circle is quilted in center of each muslin hexagon. (See page 154 for tips on making a quilting stencil from design printed on Pattern C). Borders are quilted in a 2½"-wide scalloped design. Mark quilting designs as desired.

3. Layer backing, batting, and quilt top. Backing seams will run parallel to top and bottom edges. Baste. Quilt as desired.

4. Join scrap strips to make 7¾ yards of 2½"-wide straight-grain binding. See pages 158 and 159 for instructions on making and applying binding.

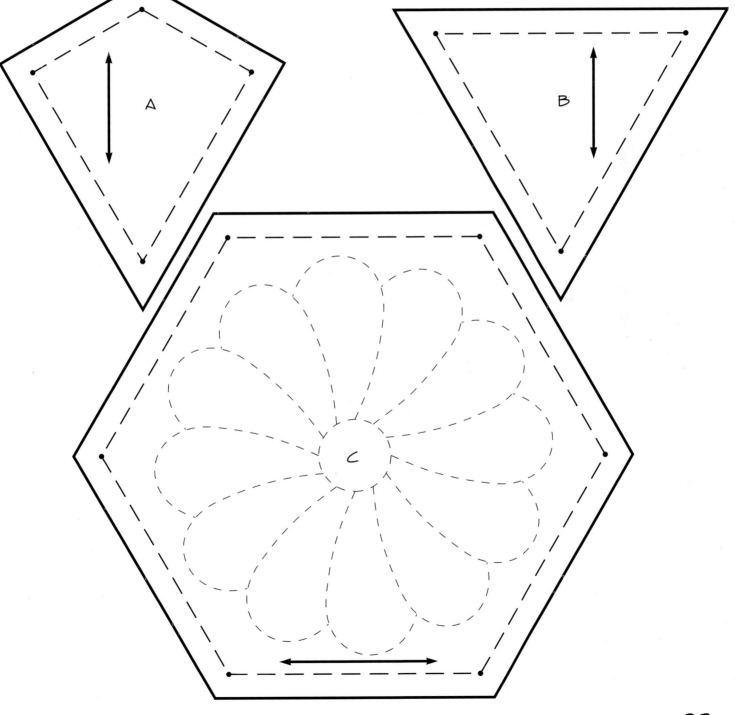

BLUEPRINTS

Piece this village of houses and be a great homemaker!
Warm hues of yellow and rust give
a glow to the windows and doors in each house of blues.

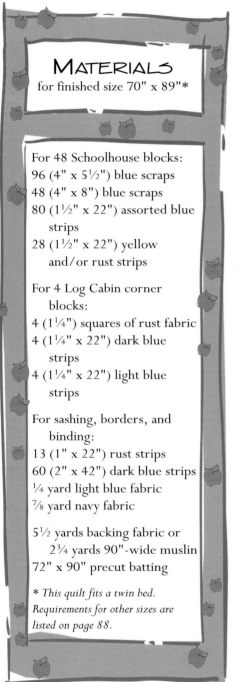

MATERIALS
for finished size 70" x 89"*

For 48 Schoolhouse blocks:
96 (4" x 5½") blue scraps
48 (4" x 8") blue scraps
80 (1½" x 22") assorted blue
    strips
28 (1½" x 22") yellow
    and/or rust strips

For 4 Log Cabin corner
    blocks:
4 (1¼") squares of rust fabric
4 (1¼" x 22") dark blue
    strips
4 (1¼" x 22") light blue
    strips

For sashing, borders, and
    binding:
13 (1" x 22") rust strips
60 (2" x 42") dark blue strips
¼ yard light blue fabric
⅞ yard navy fabric

5½ yards backing fabric or
    2¾ yards 90"-wide muslin
72" x 90" precut batting

*This quilt fits a twin bed.
Requirements for other sizes are
listed on page 88.*

CUTTING

Instructions are given for cutting angled roof and sky pieces with templates and the remaining rectangular pieces with a rotary cutter and ruler.

Make templates for patterns A, B, and C on page 88. Refer to page 144 for tips on making templates—you'll find piecing easier if you mark pivot points on these pieces. See diagrams to identify other pieces by letter.

This quilt has many pieces of similar size. Store cut pieces in zip-top plastic bags that are labeled with identifying letters.

From 4" x 5½" scraps, cut:
• 48 of Template A.
• 48 of Template C.
• 48 of Template C reversed.
• 48 (1¼" x 4") pieces for E.
  Note: Cs and E for each block are usually cut from same fabric.

From 4" x 8" scraps, cut:
• 34 of Template B.
• 14 of Template B reversed.
• 48 (1¼" x 2") pieces for D.

From assorted blue strips, cut:
• 192 (1½" x 3½") pieces for F and J.
• 96 (1½" x 4½") pieces for G.
• 96 (1½" x 5½") pieces for I.

From 1½" x 22" rust and yellow strips, cut:
• 48 (1½" x 4½") pieces for H.
• 96 (1½" x 3½") pieces for K.

From 2" x 42" dark blue strips, cut:
• 110 (2" x 8½") strips for sashing.
• 368 (2" x 4") strips for outer border.

From light blue fabric, cut:
• 63 (2") squares for sashing squares.

From navy fabric, cut:
• 1 (30") square for bias binding or 8 (2½"-wide) strips for straight-grain binding.

MAKING SCHOOLHOUSE BLOCKS

Finished size of block is 8" square. In quilt shown, 34 houses have the door on the left side, and 14 blocks have the door on the right. (See block diagrams below.) The only difference in construction is the B reversed piece in the 14 reversed blocks.

1. For each block, select 1 each of pieces A, B, C, C reversed, D, E, F, and H. Select 2 each of pieces G, I, and K, and 3 Js (Block Diagrams). (Continued)

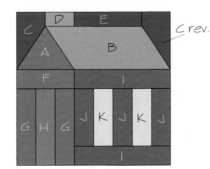

Schoolhouse Block

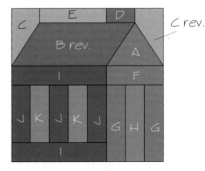

Reversed Schoolhouse Block

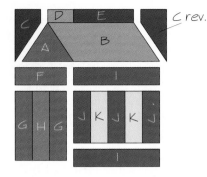

Schoolhouse Block Assembly Diagram

2. For roof section, join D to E; then join D/E to top of B (*Schoolhouse Block Assembly Diagram*). Join A to B, being careful not to sew into seam allowance at top of A. Press seam allowance toward B.

3. To set in C, first sew short side of C to D, stopping at pivot point, and backstitch. Reposition C to align diagonal edge with A. Beginning with a backstitch at pivot point, continue seam to end of A/C. Set in C reversed on opposite side in same manner.

4. For door section, join Gs to both sides of H. Join F to 1 end of unit. Press seam allowance away from F.

5. For windows section, join Js and Ks in a row as shown. Press seam allowances toward Js. Add I pieces to top and bottom edges of unit. Press seam allowances toward I pieces.

6. Join door and windows sections.

7. Join roof section to door/window section to complete block.

8. Make 34 blocks and 14 reversed blocks. Square up blocks to 8½" x 8½".

Joining Blocks

This quilt is an example of a straight set with sashing, with the blocks set 6 x 8. See setting illustration on page 149.

1. Lay out Schoolhouse blocks as desired in 8 horizontal rows, with 6 blocks in each row (*Row Assembly Diagram*). Position 7 sashing strips between blocks and at row ends as shown. When satisfied with placement, join blocks and sashing in each row. Press seam allowances toward sashing.

2. Lay out remaining sashing strips in 9 horizontal rows, with 6 strips in each row and 7 light blue squares at row ends and between strips as shown. Join strips and squares in each row. Press seam allowances toward sashing.

3. Lay out all rows, alternating sashing rows and block rows as shown in photo. Join rows.

Adding Borders

1. Referring to instructions on page 150, measure quilt from top to bottom. For each inner side border, join rust strips to achieve needed length. Join borders to quilt sides.

2. Measure quilt from side to side; then join rust strips to match quilt width. Join border to quilt top. Repeat for bottom border.

3. To make each unit for pieced border, select 2 (2" x 4") strips. With right sides facing, align pieces perpendicular to each other (*Diagram A*). Stitch a 45°-angle seam diagonally as shown. Trim excess fabric from seam allowance and press. Make 92 units with seams going same way (*Diagram A*) and another 92 units with seams going in opposite direction (*Diagram B*). Cut each unit down to 5¾" long, trimming equally from each end of unit.

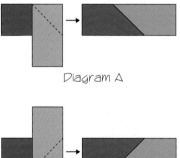

Diagram A

Diagram B

4. Join 52 pieced units for each side border, mixing seam directions of units. Join side borders to quilt. (*Note:* If pieced border doesn't fit precisely, add or subtract strips as necessary.) Press seam allowances toward inner border.

5. Join 40 pieced units each for top and bottom borders. Set aside.

Making Log Cabin Corner Blocks

To complete the house theme, the corners of the top and bottom borders are traditional Log Cabin blocks.

1. Log 1 is a 1¼" square of rust fabric (*Log Cabin Block Assembly Diagram*). For Log 2, select 1 strip of dark blue fabric. With right sides facing, stitch end of strip to square (*Diagram C*). Trim strip even with square and press.

Diagram C

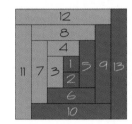

Log Cabin Block Assembly Diagram

2. With right sides facing, match a light strip to long edge of joined squares and stitch (*Diagram D*). Trim Log 3 even with bottom of unit as before and press.

Diagram D

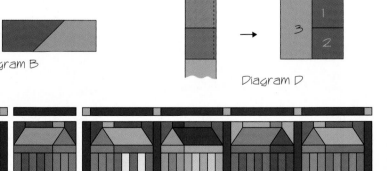

Row Assembly Diagram

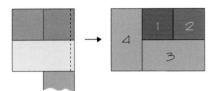

Diagram E

3. Turn unit so Log 3 is at bottom. With right sides facing, match another light strip to edge of logs 1 and 3 and stitch (Diagram E). Trim Log 4 even with bottom of unit and press.

4. Continue adding light and dark logs in this manner until you have 3 logs on all sides of center square (Log Cabin Block Assembly Diagram). Always press seam allowances toward newest log; then rotate unit to put new log at bottom to add next strip. Make 4 blocks in this manner; then square up blocks to 5¾" x 5¾".

5. Join a Log Cabin block to each end of top border. Join border to top edge of quilt, easing as necessary to fit. Repeat for bottom border. (Continued)

Quilt by Karen Kratz-Miller of Cincinnati, Ohio

FINISHING

1. Divide backing fabric into 2 (2¾-yard) lengths. Cut 1 piece in half lengthwise. Sew a narrow panel to each side of wide panel. Press seam allowances toward narrow panels.

2. Layer backing, batting, and quilt top. Baste. Quilt as desired. On quilt shown, blocks are quilted differently with horizontal, vertical, and diagonal lines that echo patchwork shapes and extend into sashing and borders. Outline-quilting is a good alternative, if desired.

3. Make 9¼ yards of bias or straight-grain binding. See pages 158 and 159 for instructions on making and applying binding.

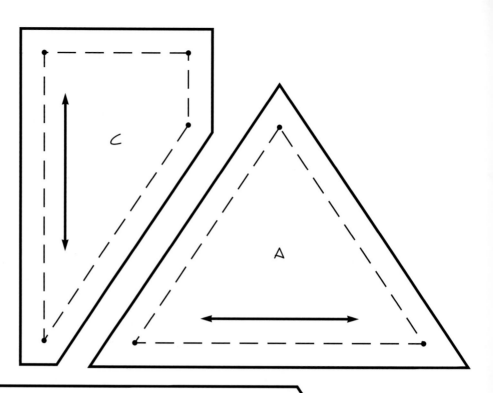

C

A

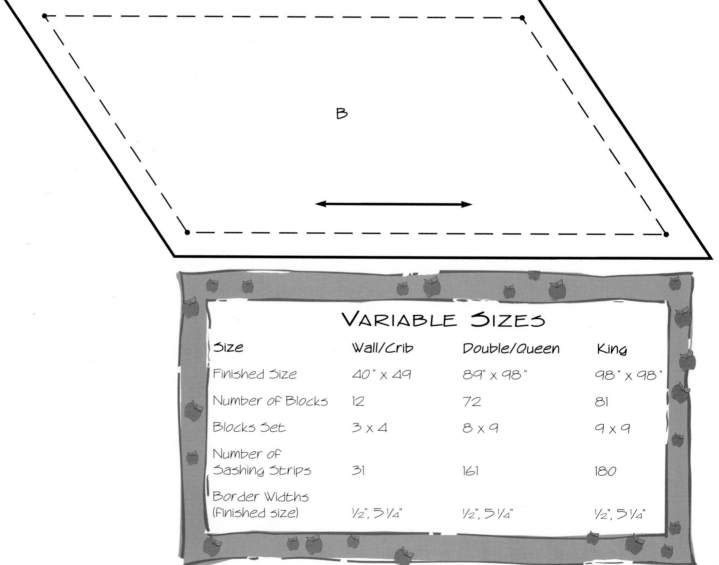

B

VARIABLE SIZES

Size	Wall/Crib	Double/Queen	King
Finished Size	40" x 49	89" x 98"	98" x 98"
Number of Blocks	12	72	81
Blocks Set	3 x 4	8 x 9	9 x 9
Number of Sashing Strips	31	161	180
Border Widths (finished size)	½", 5¼"	½", 5¼"	½", 5¼"

CHARM STARS

This quilt is doubly charming! Besides its visual appeal,
this is technically a charm quilt—one that never repeats a single
fabric. One appliquéd heart is a sweet finishing touch.

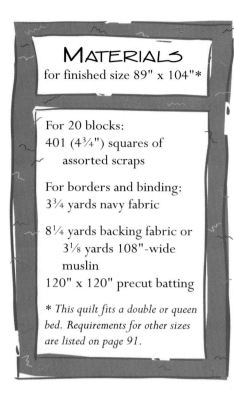

MATERIALS

for finished size 89" x 104"*

For 20 blocks:
401 (4¾") squares of
assorted scraps

For borders and binding:
3¾ yards navy fabric

8¼ yards backing fabric or
3⅛ yards 108"-wide
muslin

120" x 120" precut batting

*This quilt fits a double or queen
bed. Requirements for other sizes
are listed on page 91.*

CUTTING

Cut all strips cross-grain unless stated
otherwise.

**From *each* of 400 (4¾") squares,
cut:**
• 2 triangles by cutting each square in
half diagonally to get a total of 800.
Note: To make a true charm quilt, get
together with a group of friends and
trade triangles until each person has
800 different fabrics. That's how fabrics were collected for quilt shown.

From 1 (4¾") square, cut:
• 1 of heart appliqué pattern on page 91.
(See page 144 for tips on making a
template for appliqué.)

From navy fabric, cut:
• 1 (34") square for bias binding or 10
(2½"-wide) strips for straight-grain
binding.
• 4 (8" x 94") lengthwise strips for
outer border.
• 2 (2½" x 85") lengthwise strips and
2 (2½" x 70") lengthwise strips for
inner border.

MAKING BLOCKS

Finished size of block is 15½" square.
1. Before you select triangles for each
block, study the photo on page 91. Each
block is made of fabrics from 1 color
family. Placement of light and dark fabrics makes the stars come out. The quilt
shown has 4 blue blocks, 4 reds, 4
greens, 3 browns, 2 pinks, and 1 each of
purple, black, and turquoise.
2. Sort triangles into color groups. If
some fabrics don't blend with any group,
set these aside for placement later (like
yellows in quilt shown). Within each
group, sort lights, mediums, and darks.
From these, select 12 dark/medium
triangles and 20 light/medium triangles
for each of 20 blocks. Set aside remaining triangles for middle border.
3. For 1 block, lay out triangles in rows
to determine position (*Block Assembly
Diagram*). Place darkest fabrics at star
points and center. Position darkest
mediums around star center and remaining fabrics as desired. When satisfied
with placement, join triangles in pairs to
make squares as shown. Press squares
and trim dog-ears of triangles. Then join
squares to make 4 horizontal rows. Join
rows to complete block.

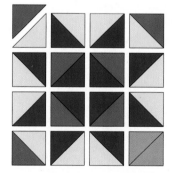

Block Assembly Diagram

4. Make 20 blocks. Square up blocks to
16" x 16".
5. Referring to quilt photo (third row,
right), appliqué heart onto 1 center
triangle of 1 block. See page 147 for
instructions on hand appliqué.

JOINING BLOCKS

This quilt is an example of a straight set,
with the blocks set 4 x 5. See setting
illustration on page 149.
1. Lay out blocks in 5 horizontal rows,
with 4 blocks in each row (*Row Assembly Diagram*). When satisfied with placement, join blocks in each row.
2. Join rows.

ADDING BORDERS

1. Referring to instructions on page
150, measure quilt from top to bottom;
then trim 2½" x 85" navy inner borders
to match length. Join borders to quilt
sides. Press seam allowances toward
borders.
2. Measure quilt from side to side;
then trim 2½" x 70" borders to match
quilt width. Join borders to top and bottom edges. Press seam allowances
toward borders.
3. For pieced border, join remaining
triangles to make 80 triangle-squares.
Referring to photo, join 21 squares in a
row for each side border and 19 squares
each for top and bottom borders. Join
side borders to quilt. Press seam allowances toward navy inner border. Join top
and bottom borders to quilt in same
manner. (*Note:* If pieced border strips
don't fit precisely, add or subtract
squares or adjust border seam allowances slightly to fit border as necessary.)

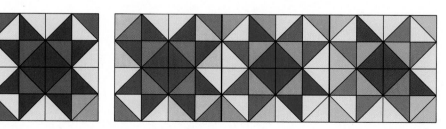

Row Assembly Diagram

Quilt by Mary Carole Sternitzky Knapp of Garfield, Arkansas

4. Measure quilt as before. Trim 8"-wide navy outer borders and join to quilt sides. Press seam allowances toward borders. Add borders to top and bottom edges in same manner.

FINISHING

1. Divide backing fabric into 3 (2¾-yard) lengths. Cut 12" off 1 piece lengthwise. Sew a wide panel to each side of narrow panel. Press seam allowances toward wide panels.

2. Quilt shown is outline-quilted, with a cable quilted in outer border. Mark desired quilting designs on quilt top.

3. Layer backing, batting, and quilt top. Backing seams will run parallel to top and bottom edges. Baste. Quilt as desired.

4. Make 11 yards of bias or straight-grain binding. See pages 158 and 159 for instructions on making and applying binding.

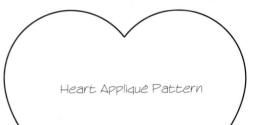

Heart Appliqué Pattern

VARIABLE SIZES

Size	Wall/Crib	Twin	King
Finished Size	43" x 43"	74" x 89½"	104" x 104"
Number of Blocks	4	12	25
Blocks Set	2 x 2	3 x 4	5 x 5
Border Widths (finished size)	2", 3⅞"	2", 3⅞", 7½"	2", 3⅞", 7½"

MILKY WAY

This patchwork galaxy plays tricks with the eye.
Pieced sashing repeats elements of the block to create
a mirage of stars within stars. The block is evident only where it stands
alone at the corners of the border.

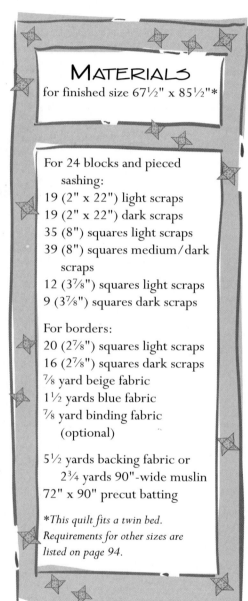

MATERIALS
for finished size 67½" x 85½"*

For 24 blocks and pieced
    sashing:
19 (2" x 22") light scraps
19 (2" x 22") dark scraps
35 (8") squares light scraps
39 (8") squares medium/dark
    scraps
12 (3⅞") squares light scraps
9 (3⅞") squares dark scraps

For borders:
20 (2⅞") squares light scraps
16 (2⅞") squares dark scraps
⅞ yard beige fabric
1½ yards blue fabric
⅞ yard binding fabric
    (optional)

5½ yards backing fabric or
    2¾ yards 90"-wide muslin
72" x 90" precut batting

*This quilt fits a twin bed.
Requirements for other sizes are
listed on page 94.

CUTTING
Cut all strips cross-grain.

From *each* 3⅞" scrap square, cut:
• 2 triangles by cutting each square in
half diagonally. These "extra" triangles
are designated by an X in *Row Assembly Diagram* on page 94.

From blue fabric, cut:
• 7 (4" x 44") strips for inner border.
• 8 (2¾" x 44") strips for outer border.

From beige fabric, cut:
• 7 (4" x 44") strips for middle border.

MAKING A PLAN
Because each star connects to another,
this quilt requires some planning to get
all the pieces in the right place. Get
organized before you begin so you won't
be confused later.

Each 8" square represents a star,
whether it's in a block or in a sashing
unit. On the floor, lay out squares in 10
horizontal rows with 7 squares in each
row. Begin odd-numbered rows with a
dark square and even-numbered rows
with a light. Referring to photo, alternate light and dark fabrics in each row.
(Four dark squares are left over for corner blocks.) Move fabrics around until
you are satisfied with placement.

Store fabrics for each row in a zip-lock
plastic bag, labelling it with the row
number. You don't have to cut those
squares until you need the pieces for
that row.

It's efficient to make all the four-patch
units at one time. Then cut and piece
remaining elements 1 row at a time.

MAKING BLOCKS AND SASHING UNITS
Finished size of block is 9" square.
1. Join each 2" x 22" light strip to a dark
strip to make 19 strip sets. Press seam
allowances toward dark fabric; then cut
11 (2"-wide) segments from each strip
set (Diagram A).
2. Join 2 segments to make a four-patch (Diagram B). Repeat to make 104
four-patches.
3. From each 8" square for Row 1, cut
2 (3⅞") squares. Cut these in half diagonally to get 4 triangles for star points.
From remaining fabric, cut 1 (3½")
square for star center and 1 (2⅞")
square. Set 2⅞" square aside with
squares for pieced border.
4. For each square and sashing unit in
Row 1, you will need 1 triangle from
stars in Row 2, so cut those squares in
same manner as for Row 1. Store cut
pieces in plastic bags to keep them
organized. *(Continued)*

Diagram A

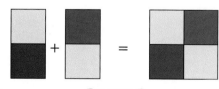

Diagram B

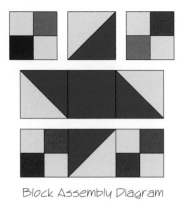

Block Assembly Diagram

Row 1

Row 2

Row 3

Row 11

Row Assembly Diagram

5. Arrange 4 triangles and 1 square for first star with 4 four-patches in 3 horizontal rows as shown (Block Assembly Diagram). In top row, fill in 1 X light triangle. (*Note:* X triangles are needed only at outside edges of patchwork. See Row Assembly Diagram.) In middle row, fill in 1 X light triangle and 1 triangle from adjacent star. In bottom row, fill in light triangle from Row 2 star.

6. Join light and dark triangles to make 4 (3½") squares. Then join squares in each row. Press seam allowances away from triangle-squares. Then join rows to complete block.

7. For sashing unit that is main part of second star, lay out 2 triangles and 1 square in a vertical row as shown (Row Assembly Diagram, Row 1). Add a dark X triangle at top and a dark triangle from Row 2 star. Join triangles; then join 3 squares to complete unit.

8. Make 3 more blocks and 2 sashing units in Row 1 in same manner. Return each completed unit to row layout to confirm fabric placement before you continue. Then join blocks and sashing units to complete Row 1.

9. Lay out pieces for Row 2. Add X triangles at ends of row as shown. Join units to complete Row 2.

10. Cut and piece blocks and sashing units for subsequent rows. Rows 3, 5, 7, and 9 are assembled in same manner as Row 1. Rows 4, 6, 8, and 10 are assembled in same manner as Row 2.

11. For symmetry, 1 extra row is required to finish stars at bottom of quilt. Join pieces for Row 11 as shown

(Row Assembly Diagram), adding X triangles as indicated.

12. When all rows are complete and you are satisfied with placement, join rows.

13. Use remaining pieces to make 4 blocks for border corners.

VARIABLE SIZES

Size	Wall/Crib	Double	Queen	King
Finished Size	39" x 51"	75" x 87"	87" x 87"	99" x 99"
Number of Stars	19	103	125	173
Number of Blocks	10	34	40	53
Blocks Set	2 x 3	5 x 6	6 x 6	7 x 7
Border Widths (finished size)	same	same	same	same

Adding Borders

1. Cut 1 (4"-wide) blue border strip in half. Join each half end-to-end with 1 full border strip to make borders for top and bottom edges. For each side, join 2 strips end-to-end. Prepare beige border strips in same manner.

2. Join each blue border to a beige border to make 4 combined border units. Press seam allowances toward blue borders.

3. Referring to instructions on page 150, measure quilt from top to bottom; then trim 2 longer border units to match length. Measure quilt from side to side and trim remaining units to match width. Do not join borders to quilt yet.

4. For pieced border, you need 55 (2⅞") light squares and 55 dark squares. Cut each square in half diagonally to get 2 triangles. Join each light triangle to a dark triangle to make 110 (2½") triangle-squares.

5. For each side border, join 32 triangle-squares in a row (Diagram C), always sewing dark fabrics to darks and lights to lights. Join dark side of pieced border to beige border strip, easing to fit as necessary. (*Note:* If pieced border doesn't fit precisely, add or subtract squares as needed.) Join completed border strips to quilt sides. Press seam allowances toward borders.

Diagram C

6. For top border, join 23 triangle-squares. Sew pieced border to beige border strip as for side borders. Prepare bottom border in same manner.

7. Join corner blocks to both ends of top and bottom borders; then join borders to top and bottom edges.

Finishing

1. Divide backing fabric into 2 (2¾-yard) lengths. Cut 1 piece in half lengthwise. Sew a narrow panel to each side of wide panel. Press seam allowances toward narrow panels.

2. Mark desired quilting designs on quilt top. On quilt shown, patchwork is outline-quilted and a twisted cable is quilted in blue and beige borders.

3. Layer backing, batting, and quilt top. Baste. Quilt as desired.

4. Trim backing even with quilt top. Turn under raw edges and hem with a blindstitch. If you prefer, make 9 yards of bias or straight-grain binding. See pages 158 and 159 for instructions on making and applying binding.

Quilt made by Judy Chiodini of St. Louis, Missouri, and quilted by Tillie Plouder

IRISH CHAIN

Strip piecing makes this all-time favorite so fast and so fun that it's better than ever. The same techniques will produce a classic whether your scraps are Easter-egg pastels or dramatic jewel tones.

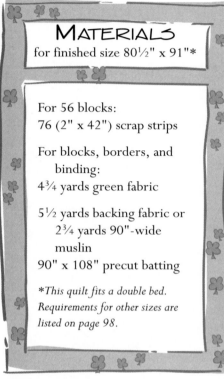

MATERIALS

for finished size 80½" x 91"*

For 56 blocks:
76 (2" x 42") scrap strips

For blocks, borders, and
    binding:
4¾ yards green fabric

5½ yards backing fabric or
    2¾ yards 90"-wide
    muslin
90" x 108" precut batting

*This quilt fits a double bed.
Requirements for other sizes are
listed on page 98.*

CUTTING

Cut all strips cross-grain unless stated
otherwise.

From green fabric, cut:
• 2 (4" x 85") lengthwise strips and
  2 (4" x 95") lengthwise strips for
  border.
• 28 (8") squares for B blocks.
• 1 (32") square for bias binding or 9
  (2½"-wide) strips for straight-grain
  binding.
• 6 (5"-wide) strips. From these, cut
  16 (5" x 14") strips for strip sets 4
  and 5.
• 16 (2" x 14") strips for strip sets 1
  and 2.

From *each* scrap strip, cut:
• 3 (14"-long) strips to get a total of 228
  scrap strips.

MAKING BLOCKS

Finished size of blocks is 10½" square.
Two blocks alternate to create the illusion of a continuous chain.

1. For Strip Set 1, select 1 (2" x 14")
green strip and 6 scrap strips. Join scrap
strips in 2 groups of 3 (*Strip Set 1
Diagram*); then join each group to opposite sides of green strip. Press all seam
allowances toward center green strip.
Make 8 of Strip Set 1.

2. For Strip Set 2, select 2 (2" x 14")
green strips and 5 scrap strips. Join
scrap strips (*Strip Set 2 Diagram*); then
join green strips to top and bottom
edges. Press all seam allowances outward from center, toward green strips.
Make 4 of Strip Set 2.

3. For Strip Set 3, join 7 scrap strips.
Make 16 of Strip Set 3. In 8 of these,

press seam allowances toward center
strip. In 8 remaining strip sets, press
seam allowances away from center strip.

4. From each strip set, cut 7 (2"-wide)
segments for Block A, cutting 56 from
Strip Set 1, 28 from Strip Set 2, and 112
from Strip Set 3.

5. For Strip Set 4, select 1 (5" x 14")
green strip and 4 scrap strips. Join scrap
strips in pairs (*Strip Set 4 Diagram*);
then join each pair to opposite sides of
green strip. Press all seam allowances
outward from center, away from green
strip. Make 8 of Strip Set 4.

6. For Strip Set 5, select 1 (5" x 14")
green strip and 2 scrap strips. Join scrap
strips to opposite sides of green strip
(*Strip Set 5 Diagram*). Press all seam
allowances toward green strip. Make 8
of Strip Set 5.   (Continued)

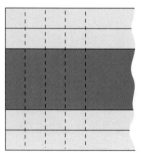

Strip Set 1
Diagram—Make 8.

Strip Set 4
Diagram—Make 8.

Strip Set 2
Diagram—Make 4.

Strip Set 5
Diagram—Make 8.

7. For each A block, select 2 segments from Strip Set 1, 1 from Strip Set 2, and 4 from Strip Set 3. Arrange segments as shown (*Block A Assembly Diagram*), and check to see that seam allowances offset from row to row. If not, substitute another Strip Set 3 segment as needed. When satisfied with placement, join 7 rows to complete Block A. Make 28 of Block A.

8. For each B block, select 1 (8") square, 2 segments from Strip Set 4, and 2 segments from Strip Set 5. Arrange segments as shown (*Block B Assembly Diagram*). Join Strip Set 5 segments to sides of square as shown, and press seam allowances toward green square. Then join Strip Set 4 segments to complete Block B. Make 28 of Block B.

JOINING BLOCKS

This quilt is an example of a straight set with alternating blocks. The blocks are set 7 x 8. See setting illustration on page 149.

1. Lay out 8 horizontal rows of 7 blocks each, alternating A blocks and B blocks (*Row Assembly Diagram*). Lay out 4 of Row 1, starting with an A block. Then lay out 4 of Row 2, starting with a B block. Turn blocks as necessary to offset seam allowances. When satisfied with placement, join blocks in each row.

2. Join rows, alternating rows as shown in photo.

ADDING BORDERS

1. Read instructions for mitered borders on pages 150 and 151.

2. Measure length of quilt; then mark 2 longer border strips to match length. Measure width of quilt and mark 2 remaining borders to match width. Join borders to quilt. Press seam allowances toward borders. Miter corners.

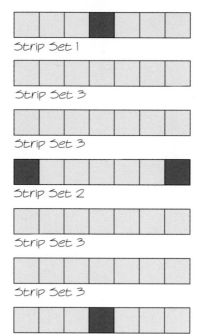

Strip Set 1

Strip Set 3

Strip Set 3

Strip Set 2

Strip Set 3

Strip Set 3

Strip Set 1

Block A Assembly Diagram

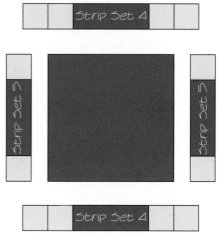

Strip Set 4

Strip Set 5

Strip Set 5

Strip Set 4

Block B Assembly Diagram

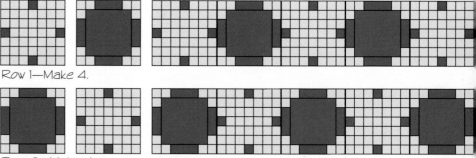

Row 1—Make 4.

Row 2—Make 4.

Row Assembly Diagram

VARIABLE SIZES

Size	Twin	Queen	King
Finished Size	59½" x 91"	91" x 91"	101" x 101"
Number of Blocks			
A	20	32	41
B	20	32	40
Blocks Set	5 x 8	8 x 8	9 x 9

FINISHING

1. Divide backing fabric into 2 (2¾-yard) lengths. Cut 1 piece in half lengthwise. Sew a narrow panel to each side of wide panel. Press seam allowances toward narrow panels.

2. On quilt shown, diagonal lines are quilted in small squares and a sunflower is quilted in center square of each B block. Two other quilting sugggestions are shown here (Alternate Quilting Diagrams). Mark desired quilting designs on quilt top.

3. Layer backing, batting, and quilt top. Baste. Quilt as desired.

4. Make 10 yards of bias or straight-grain binding. See pages 158 and 159 for instructions on making and applying binding.

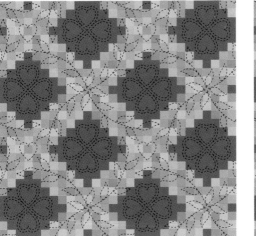 

Alternate Quilting Diagrams

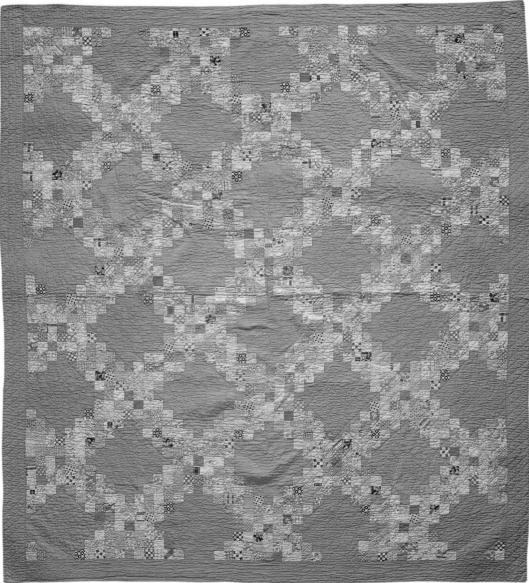

Antique quilt owned by Susie Braund of Madison, Alabama

REUNION STAR

This quilt is the outcome of a challenge to use elements from one block to make a completely new one. The result is an expanded red star that casts halos of light around traditional blue stars.

MATERIALS
for finished size 56" x 68"*

For 10 Star blocks and
    10 Expanded Star blocks:
280 (2½") squares tan scraps
40 (2¾" x 5⅜") navy scraps
40 (2¾" x 5⅜") red scraps
80 (2¾" x 5⅜") tan scraps
40 (2½" x 4½") tan scraps
10 (4½") squares navy/tan
    print scraps

For border and binding:
88 (2½") squares tan scraps
9 (2¾" x 5⅜") navy scraps
9 (2¾" x 5⅜") red scraps
18 (2¾" x 5⅜") tan scraps
⅜ yard beige fabric
¾ yard blue fabric for
    binding

3½ yards backing fabric
72" x 90" precut batting

*This quilt is a wall hanging or
lap quilt. Requirements for larger
sizes are listed on page 103.*

CUTTING

Cut all strips cross-grain.

From *each* 2¾" x 5⅜" scrap, cut:

• 2 triangles by cutting each rectangle in
half diagonally. For each color, cut half
the rectangles in 1 direction and half in
the other (Diagram A). Store each
group separately. Cut a total of 98
navy triangles, 98 red triangles, and
196 tan triangles. For ease of piecing,
trim ⅞" from top of each triangle.

From beige fabric, cut:

• 4 (2½"-wide) strips. From these, cut
18 (2½" x 8½") strips for border.

From blue fabric, cut:

• 1 (27") square for bias binding or 7
(2½"-wide) strips for straight-grain
binding.

MAKING STAR BLOCKS

Finished size of block is 12" square.

1. For each block, select 20 tan squares, 8
tan triangles, and 8 navy triangles, selecting half the triangles from each group.

2. Join squares in pairs; then join pairs
to make 5 four-patch units (Diagram B).

3. Join navy and tan triangles to make 8
rectangles. Join rectangles in pairs to
make 4 (4½") squares (Diagram C). Press
seam allowances toward navy triangles.

4. Lay out 9 units in 3 horizontal rows
(Star Block Diagram). Join units in each
row; then join rows to complete block.

5. Make 10 Star blocks. Square up
blocks to 12½" x 12½".

MAKING EXPANDED STAR BLOCKS

Finished size of block is 12" square.

1. For each block, select 1 navy/tan print
square, 8 tan squares, 4 (2½" x 4½") tan
strips, 8 tan triangles, and 8 red triangles.
Select half the triangles from each group.

2. Join tan and red triangles as for Star
blocks, making 8 rectangles. Press seam
allowances toward red fabric. Join rectangles in pairs, joining ends of tan triangles (Expanded Star Block Diagram).

3. Join 2 tan strips to opposite sides of
navy/tan print square. Press seam allowances toward square.

4. Join tan squares to ends of remaining
tan strips. Press seam allowances toward
squares. Join these to red sides of 2 triangle units as shown; then join combined units to sides of center square.

5. Join tan squares to ends of remaining triangle units. Sew these to top and
bottom edges to complete block.

6. Make 10 Expanded Star blocks.
Square up blocks to 12½" x 12½".

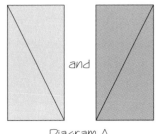

Diagram A

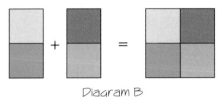

Diagram B

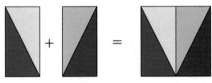

Diagram C

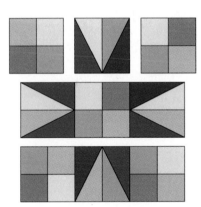

Star Block Diagram

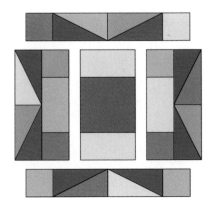

Expanded Star Block Diagram

Making Border Units

1. Join remaining 18 red triangles to tan triangles to make rectangles. Join rectangles in pairs end to end (*Diagram D*). Add a tan square to both ends of each unit. Press seam allowances toward squares.

2. Join a tan square to both ends of 9 (2½" x 8½") beige strips. Press seam allowances toward strips.

3. Join strip unit to top (red) edge of each triangle unit as shown. Make 9 red border units.

4. Join blue triangle units and strip units (*Diagram E*). Assemble 9 blue border units, joining strip units to bottom (tan) edge of triangle units as shown.

5. Use remaining tan squares to make 4 four-patch units for border corners.

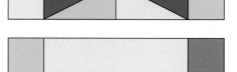

Diagram D

Diagram E

Quilt by Marjean K. Sargent of Malvern, Iowa

JOINING BLOCKS

This quilt is an example of a straight set with alternating blocks. The blocks in this horizontal wall hanging are set 5 x 4 and are surrounded by pieced border units. See setting illustration on page 149.

1. For Row 1, lay out 2 red border units and 2 blue border units in a vertical row with a corner four-patch at each end (Row Assembly Diagram). For Row 2, lay out a row of 2 Star blocks and 2 Expanded Star blocks, adding 1 border unit at each end of row as shown. For Row 3, alternate positions of blocks as shown; then add border units. Referring to photo, lay out blocks for rows 4, 5, 6, and 7 in same manner.

2. When satisfied with placement, join blocks in each row. Join rows to complete quilt.

FINISHING

1. Divide backing fabric into 2 (1¾-yard) lengths. Cut 1 piece in half lengthwise. Sew a narrow panel to each side of wide panel. Press seam allowances toward narrow panels.

2. Layer backing, batting, and quilt top. Baste. Quilt as desired. On quilt shown, straight-line quilting accentuates circles of light fabrics.

3. Make 7¼ yards of bias or straight-grain binding. See pages 158 and 159 for instructions on making and applying binding.

4. See page 23 for tips on making a hanging sleeve, if desired.

Row 1   Row 2   Row 3

Row Assembly Diagram

VARIABLE SIZES

Size	Twin	Double/Queen	King
Finished Size	68" x 80"	80" x 92"	92" x 92"
Number of Blocks			
Star	15	21	24
Expanded Star	15	21	25
Blocks Set	5 x 6	6 x 7	7 x 7

KANSAS TROUBLES

Almost totally triangles, this quilt is a triumph of geometry!
You'll love how fast your rotary cutter turns scraps
into ready-to-sew pieces for this super scrap celebration.

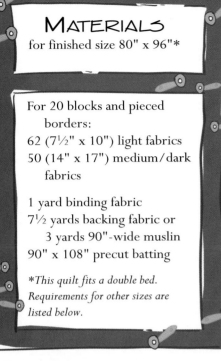

MATERIALS

for finished size 80" x 96"*

For 20 blocks and pieced
borders:
62 (7½" x 10") light fabrics
50 (14" x 17") medium/dark
   fabrics

1 yard binding fabric
7½ yards backing fabric or
   3 yards 90"-wide muslin
90" x 108" precut batting

*This quilt fits a double bed.
Requirements for other sizes are
listed below.*

CUTTING

Cut larger pieces first, as listed; then cut
smaller pieces from leftover fabric.

Refer to diagrams to identify each
piece by letter designation. This quilt
has many triangles of similar size. To be
sure you select the correct piece to sew,
store cut pieces in zip-top plastic bags
that are labeled with identifying letters.

From light scraps, cut:

• 59 (7") squares for D and H triangle-
   squares.
• 1 (3⅞") square. Cut this in quarters
   diagonally to get 4 extra H triangles
   for border.
• 40 (2½") C squares.
• 164 (2⅜") I squares for borders.

From binding fabric, cut:

• 1 (32") square for bias binding or 9
   (2½"-wide) strips for straight-grain
   binding.

From medium/dark scraps, cut:

• 9 (9¼") squares. Cut these in quarters
   diagonally to get a total of 36 E triangles for border.
• 40 (8⅞") squares. Cut these in half
   diagonally to get 80 A triangles.
• 59 (7") squares for D and H triangle-
   squares.
• 9 (6⅝") squares. Cut these in quarters
   diagonally to get a total of 36 F triangles for border.
• 2 (6¼") squares. Cut these in half
   diagonally to get 4 J triangles for
   border.
• 40 (4⅞") squares. Cut these in half
   diagonally to get 80 B triangles.
• 74 (3⅞") squares. Cut these in quarters diagonally to get 260 H triangles
   for borders.
• 2 (3½") squares. Cut these in half diagonally to get 4 G triangles for border.
• 80 (2⅞") squares. Cut these in half
   diagonally to get 160 extra D
   triangles.

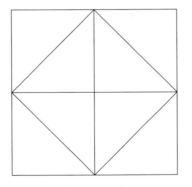

Diagram A

MAKING BLOCKS

Finished size of block is 16" square.

1. Select 40 (7") light squares for D
triangle-squares. On wrong side of each
square, draw a 2 x 2 grid of 2⅞" squares
(Diagram A), leaving a small margin of
fabric around drawing. Draw diagonal
lines through squares as shown. With
right sides facing, match 1 marked
square with 1 (7") dark square. Stitch
¼" seam on *both* sides of diagonal lines
(Diagram B). Press. Cut on all drawn
lines to get 8 triangle-squares. Repeat
with each set of light/dark squares to
get a total of 320 D triangle-squares.
Press seam allowances toward scrap fabric; then trim points. (Continued)

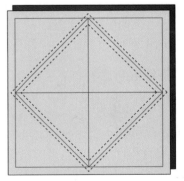

Diagram B

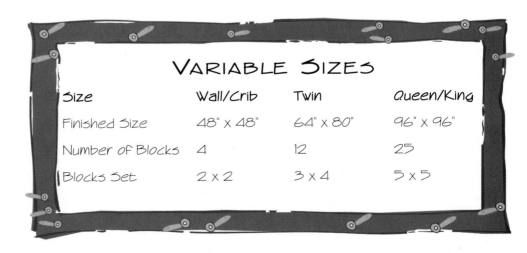

VARIABLE SIZES

Size	Wall/Crib	Twin	Queen/King
Finished Size	48" x 48"	64" x 80"	96" x 96"
Number of Blocks	4	12	25
Blocks Set	2 x 2	3 x 4	5 x 5

2. For each quarter-block, select 1 each of A, B, and C, plus 4 D triangle-squares and 2 extra D triangles. Join triangle-squares in pairs, sewing light sides to dark sides as shown (Diagram C). Join 1 extra D triangle to light end of each pair. Press seam allowances toward dark fabrics.

3. Sew 1 triangle-square unit to 1 leg of B triangle (Diagram C); then press seam allowance toward B. Join C square to dark end of second triangle-square unit. Press seam allowance toward C; then join unit to remaining leg of B triangle. Press; then join A triangle as shown to complete quarter-block.

4. Make 80 quarter-block units, 4 for each block. Each quarter block should be approximately 8½" square.

5. Select 4 quarter-blocks for each block. Join units in pairs, sewing A triangle of 1 unit to D triangle-square edge of second unit (Block Assembly Diagram). Join pairs as shown to complete block.

6. Make 20 Kansas Troubles blocks. Square up blocks to 16½" x 16½".

JOINING BLOCKS

This quilt is an example of a straight set, with the blocks set 4 x 5 and surrounded by pieced borders. See setting illustration on page 149.

1. Lay out 5 horizontal rows, with 4 blocks in each row (Row Assembly Diagram). When satisfied with placement, join blocks in each row.

2. Join rows as shown in photo.

MAKING INNER BORDER

1. Use remaining 7" squares to make H triangle-squares. Make these in same manner as for D triangle-squares, this time drawing a 2 x 2 grid of 2¾" squares.

Stitch on 19 light/dark square pairs; press. Then cut out 152 triangle-squares.

2. For each border unit, select 1 each of E, F, and I, plus 4 H triangle-squares and 1 extra H triangle. Join triangle-squares in pairs, sewing light sides to dark sides as shown (Border Unit Diagram).

3. Join extra H triangle to light end of 1 triangle-square pair. Press seam allowances toward dark fabrics. Sew this to 1 leg of F triangle as shown; then press seam allowance toward F. Join I square to remaining triangle-square pair and press seam allowances toward I. Join this to 1 leg of E triangle as shown; then press seam allowance toward E. Join

halves to complete border unit. Make 34 border units.

4. Select 7 border units for top border, 7 for bottom border, and 10 for each side border.

5. For top border, join 7 border units in a row as shown (Top Border Diagram). Make 2 corner units as shown (Diagram D), using G triangles and light H triangles. Join these to ends of border as shown. Make bottom border in same manner. Join borders to top and bottom edges of quilt, easing as necessary. If borders don't fit quilt, add or subtract border units as desired.

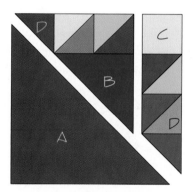

Diagram C

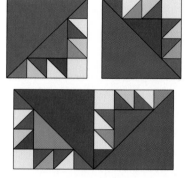

Block Assembly Diagram

Row Assembly Diagram

Border Unit Diagram—Make 34.

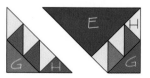

Diagram D

Corner Unit ← | Top Border Diagram | → Corner Unit

6. For each side border, join 10 border units in a row in same manner. For each border, make 1 corner unit as shown (Diagram E), using 1 J triangle. Join this unit to left end of side border (Side Border Diagram); then join another J triangle to right end of border. Join borders to sides of quilt, easing as needed.

MAKING OUTER BORDER

1. For top border, select 29 I squares and 58 H triangles. Referring to photo, lay out pieces in a row. Starting at left corner, sew a triangle to 2 adjacent sides of first square (Diagram F). For remaining squares in row, sew triangles to opposite edges as shown. Press seam allowances toward squares. Join units in a row as shown. Assemble bottom border in same manner.

2. Matching centers, join pieced borders to top and bottom edges of quilt. Press seam allowances toward inner border. Trim borders even with quilt sides.

3. Use 35 squares and 70 triangles to assemble each side border. Matching centers, join borders to quilt sides. Trim borders as needed.

FINISHING

1. Divide backing fabric into 3 (2½-yard) lengths. Cut 1 piece in half lengthwise. Discard 1 narrow panel. Sew wide panels to each side of remaining narrow panel. Press seam allowances toward wide panels.

2. Layer backing, batting, and quilt top. Backing seams will run parallel to top and bottom edges. Baste. Quilt as desired. On quilt shown, patchwork is outline-quilted with cross-hatching filling largest triangles.

3. Make 10¼ yards of bias or straight-grain binding. See pages 158 and 159 for instructions on making and applying binding.

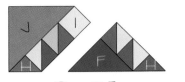

Diagram E

Diagram F

Corner Unit

Side Border Diagram

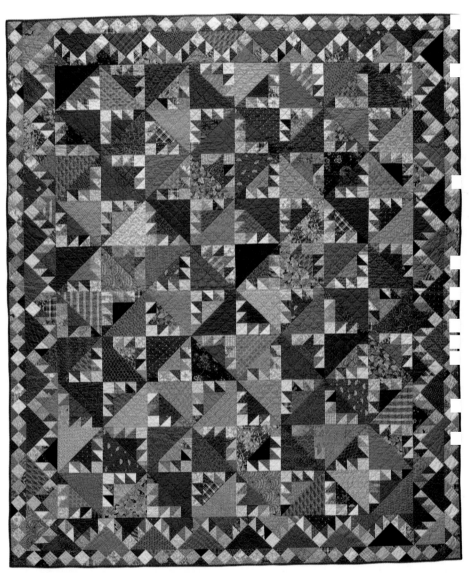

Quilt by Marion Roach Watchinski of Overland Park, Kansas

STAR PATH

If you think there are two different blocks in this quilt, the patchwork is playing a trick on you! All the blocks are the same, so paths and stars are created by turning adjacent blocks. A pieced inner border cleverly completes the illusion.

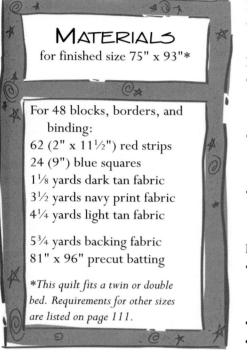

MATERIALS
for finished size 75" x 93"*

For 48 blocks, borders, and
   binding:
62 (2" x 11½") red strips
24 (9") blue squares
1⅛ yards dark tan fabric
3½ yards navy print fabric
4¼ yards light tan fabric

5¾ yards backing fabric
81" x 96" precut batting

This quilt fits a twin or double bed. Requirements for other sizes are listed on page 111.

CUTTING

Cut all strips cross-grain unless stated otherwise.

To mark matching points, make a template for the X diamond even if you prefer to cut pieces with a rotary cutter. (See page 144, steps 2 and 5, for tips on making templates and marking matching points.) Pattern for diamond is on page 111. Instructions are given for cutting X diamonds with template or with a rotary cutter and ruler.

From *each* red strip, cut:
• 4 X diamonds. From 31 strips, cut with template right side up; then cut with template facedown on remaining strips to get a total of 124 X diamonds and 124 X reversed diamonds. *Mark matching points on each piece.* If you prefer to rotary-cut without using a template, see Diagram A.

From dark tan fabric, cut:
• 3 (18") squares for A triangle-squares.

From navy print fabric, cut:
• 2 (5½" x 80") lengthwise strips and 2 (5½" x 88") lengthwise strips for outer border.
• 1 (32") square for bias binding or 9 (2½"-wide) strips for straight-grain binding.
• 4 (18") squares for A and D triangle-squares.

From light tan fabric, cut:
• 2 (3" x 69") lengthwise strips and 2 (3" x 82") lengthwise strips for middle border.
• 1 (18") square for D triangle-squares.
• 24 (9") squares for B triangle-squares.
• 76 (3½") C squares.
• 124 (2") Y squares.
• 124 (2⅜") squares. Cut each of these in half diagonally to get a total of 248 Z triangles.

MAKING BLOCKS

Finished size of block is 9" square.

1. With right sides facing, pair 1 X diamond and 1 X reversed diamond. Starting at 1 matching point, join diamonds along 1 long side, sewing from dot to dot to leave seam allowances free at ends of seam (Diagram B). Press seam allowances to 1 side.

2. Using a ruler to measure ¼" seam allowance, mark matching points on 1 Y square. With right sides facing, pin Y square to edge of 1 diamond, aligning matching points (Diagram C). Starting at outside edge, machine-stitch from dot to dot. Backstitch at corner and clip thread. Realign pieces to pin adjacent side of Y to second diamond (Diagram D). Starting at corner dot, stitch from matching point to outside edge.

3. Complete unit by adding 2 Z triangles (Diagram E). Make 124 X/Y/Z units, 2 for each block and 1 for each border unit. (continued)

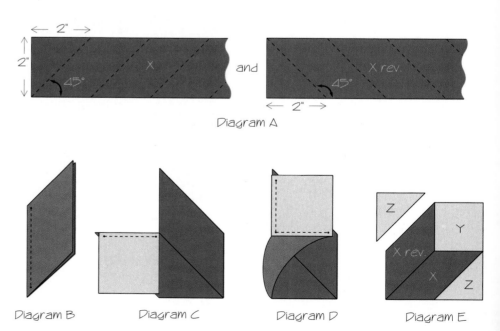

Diagram A

Diagram B   Diagram C   Diagram D   Diagram E

4. For A triangle-squares, draw a 4 x 4 grid of 3⅞" squares on wrong side of an 18" square of dark tan fabric (Diagram F), leaving a small margin of fabric around drawing. Draw diagonal lines through squares as shown. With right sides facing, match tan square with 1 (18") navy square. Stitch ¼" seam on *both* sides of diagonal lines (Diagram G). Press. Cut on all drawn lines to get 32 A triangle-squares. Press seam allowances toward navy fabric and trim triangle points. Repeat with 2 more pairs of dark tan and navy squares to get a total of 96 A triangle-squares.

5. On wrong side of each light tan square, draw a 2 x 2 grid of 3⅞" squares (Diagram H), leaving a small margin of fabric around drawing. Draw diagonal lines through squares as shown. With right sides facing, match 1 marked square with 1 (9") blue square. Stitch ¼" seam on *both* sides of diagonal lines. Press. Cut on all drawn lines to get 8 triangle-squares. Repeat with all tan and scrap squares to get a total of 192 B triangle-squares. Press seam allowances toward scrap fabric; then trim points.

6. For each block, select 2 A triangle-squares, 4 B triangle-squares, 1 C square, and 2 X/Y/Z units. Arrange units in 3 horizontal rows (Block Assembly Diagram). Join units in each row; then join rows to complete block.

7. Make 48 blocks. Square up blocks to 9½" x 9½".

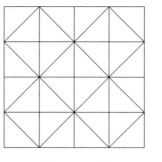

Diagram F

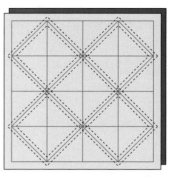

Diagram G

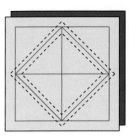

Diagram H

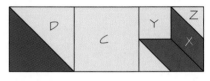

Border Unit A Diagram—Make 14.

Block Assembly Diagram

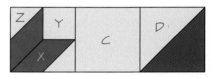

Border Unit B Diagram—Make 14.

Row 1—Make 2.

Row 2—Make 4.

Row 3—Make 4.

Row Assembly Diagram

MAKING BORDER UNITS

1. Use remaining 18" squares of navy and light tan fabrics to make 32 D triangle-squares in same manner as for A triangle-squares. Set aside 4 of these for border corner units.

2. For each border unit, select 1 D triangle-square, 1 X/Y/Z unit, and 1 C square. Join 3 units in a row (Border Unit Diagrams). Make 14 of Border Unit A and 14 of Border Unit B.

JOINING BLOCKS

This quilt is an example of a straight set. The blocks are set 6 x 8 and surrounded by a pieced border that completes the red stars around the outer edge. See illustration of a straight set on page 149.

1. For Row 1, lay out 6 border units in a row with a corner unit at each end (Row Assembly Diagram), alternating 3 Border Unit As and 3 Border Unit Bs as shown. Lay out 2 of Row 1.

2. Lay out blocks in 8 horizontal rows

of 6 blocks each. Lay out 4 of Row 2 as shown, alternating direction of blocks across row; then add border units at ends of rows as shown. Then lay out blocks and border units for 4 of Row 3 in same manner.

3. When satisfied with placement, join blocks in each row.

4. Join block rows, alternating rows 2 and 3 as shown in photo. Sew 1 of Row 1 to top of quilt. Turn second Row 1 upside down and join it to bottom of quilt.

Quilt by Ann Winterton Seely of Salt Lake City, Utah

ADDING BORDERS

1. Referring to instructions on page 150, measure quilt from top to bottom; then trim longer tan borders to match length. Join borders to quilt sides.

2. Measure quilt from side to side; then trim remaining tan borders to match quilt width. Join borders to top and bottom edges.

3. Measure and sew navy border strips to quilt in same manner.

FINISHING

1. Divide backing fabric into 2 ($2\frac{7}{8}$-yard) lengths. Cut 1 piece in half lengthwise. Sew a narrow panel to each side of wide panel.

2. Mark desired quilting designs on quilt top. Quilt shown is outline-quilted to accentuate red stars.

3. Layer backing, batting, and quilt top. Baste. Quilt as desired.

4. Make $9\frac{3}{4}$ yards of $2\frac{1}{2}$"-wide bias or straight-grain binding. See pages 158 and 159 for instructions on making and applying binding.

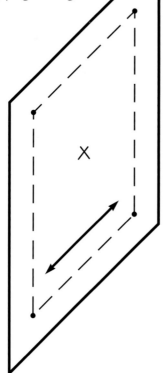

VARIABLE SIZES

Size	Wall/Crib	Queen	King
Finished Size	39" x 57"	93" x 93"	111" x 111"
Number of Blocks	8	64	100
Blocks Set	2 x 4	8 x 8	10 x 10
Number of Border Units	12	32	40
Border Widths (finished size)	$2\frac{1}{2}$", 5"	$2\frac{1}{2}$", 5"	$2\frac{1}{2}$", 5"

DAHLIA DELIGHT

Consistency and variety combine to give this quilt an orderly vigor. Pieced sashing defines the blocks like neat flower beds. All the appliquéd posies are zesty scrap fabrics, but the golden flower centers are uniform.

MATERIALS
for finished size 81" x 92½"

For appliqué:
84 (8" x 10") scraps
½ yard dark gold fabric
¼ yard light gold fabric

For 42 blocks, borders, and binding:
3⅝ yards beige print fabric
1½ yards medium green fabric
2½ yards dark green fabric
Nonpermanent fabric marker

6 yards backing fabric or
    3 yards 90"-wide muslin
90" x 108" precut batting

* This quilt fits a double or queen bed. Requirements for other sizes are listed on page 114.

CUTTING

Before cutting, choose an appliqué technique. Directions on cutting pieces for hand appliqué are on page 144. Make templates for patterns A–D on page 115. Add seam allowance when cutting fabric.

Cut all strips cross-grain unless stated otherwise.

From scraps, cut:
• 168 A petals in sets of 4.
• 168 B petals in sets of 4.

From dark gold fabric, cut:
• 42 C circles.

From light gold fabric, cut:
• 42 D circles.

From beige fabric, cut:
• 4 (5½" x 88") lengthwise strips for borders.
• 42 (10") squares.

From medium green fabric, cut:
• 49 (1"-wide) strips for sashing.

From dark green fabric, cut:
• 25 (1½"-wide) strips for sashing.
• 1 (32") square for bias binding or 9 (2½"-wide) strips for straight-grain binding.
• 56 (2½") squares for sashing.

MAKING BLOCKS

Finished size of block is 9½" square.
1. Fold each beige square in half diagonally, vertically, and horizontally, finger-pressing a crease in each direction for placement guides. Position square over printed dahlia pattern, matching center of square with marked center of pattern. Lightly trace outline of pattern onto square.
2. For each block, select 4 A petals of the same fabric and 4 B petals of 1 contrasting fabric. Prepare petals for appliqué. Directions on preparing pieces for hand appliqué are on page 147.
3. Position A petals on square, aligning points of petals with diagonal placement lines. Appliqué.

4. Position B petals, aligning points with horizontal and vertical placement lines. Appliqué.
5. Prepare C and D circles for appliqué. Appliqué 1 D to each C to make 42 center units. Appliqué 1 unit to center of each flower, making sure center unit covers bottom edges of petals. Complete appliqué for 42 blocks.

MAKING SASHING

1. Join 1 strip of medium green fabric to both sides of 24 dark green strips (*Strip Set Diagram*) to make 24 strip sets. Cut remaining strips in half and sew both medium green strips to both sides of 1 dark green strip to make 1 short strip set. (Add remaining dark green strip to scrap bag.) Press all seam allowances toward darker fabric.

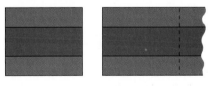

Strip Set Diagram

2. Cut each strip set into 10"-wide segments for sashing (*Strip Set Diagram*).

(Continued)

JOINING BLOCKS

This quilt is an example of a straight set with sashing, with the blocks set 6 x 7. See setting illustration on page 149.

1. Lay out blocks in 7 horizontal rows, with 6 blocks in each row (*Row Assembly Diagram*). Position 7 sashing strips between blocks and at ends of row as shown. When satisfied with placement, join blocks and sashing in each row. Press seam allowances toward sashing.

2. Lay out remaining sashing strips in 8 horizontal rows, with 6 strips in each row and 7 (2½") squares between strips and at ends of row. Join strips and squares in each row. Press seam allowances toward sashing.

3. Lay out all rows, alternating block rows and sashing rows as shown in photo. Join rows. Press seam allowances toward sashing rows.

ADDING BORDERS

1. Referring to instructions on page 150, measure quilt from top to bottom; then trim 2 borders to match length. Join borders to quilt sides. Press seam allowances toward borders.

2. Measure quilt from side to side; then trim border to match quilt width. Join borders to top and bottom edges. Press seam allowances toward borders.

FINISHING

1. Divide backing fabric into 2 (3-yard) lengths. Cut 1 piece in half lengthwise. Sew a narrow panel to each side of wide panel. Press seam allowances toward narrow panels.

2. On quilt shown, dahlias are echo-quilted and a swag design is quilted in the border. Mark desired quilting designs on quilt top.

3. Layer backing, batting, and quilt top. Baste. Quilt as desired.

4. Make 10 yards of bias or straight-grain binding. See pages 158 and 159 for instructions on making and applying binding.

Row Assembly Diagram

VARIABLE SIZES

Size	Wall/Crib	Twin	King
Finished Size	46½" x 46½"	69½" x 92½"	92½" x 104"
Number of Blocks	9	35	56
Blocks Set	3 x 3	5 x 7	7 x 8
Border Width (finished size)	5"	5"	5"

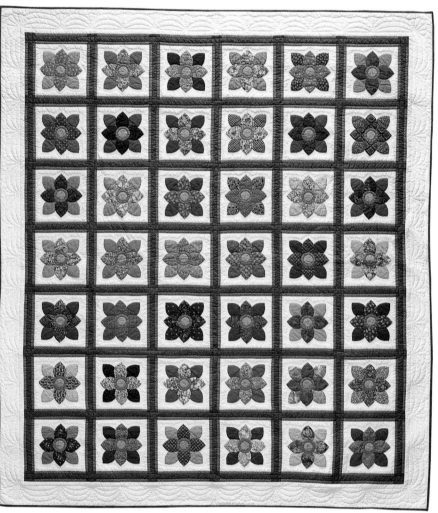

Quilt by Lyn Johnson of Columbia, South Carolina

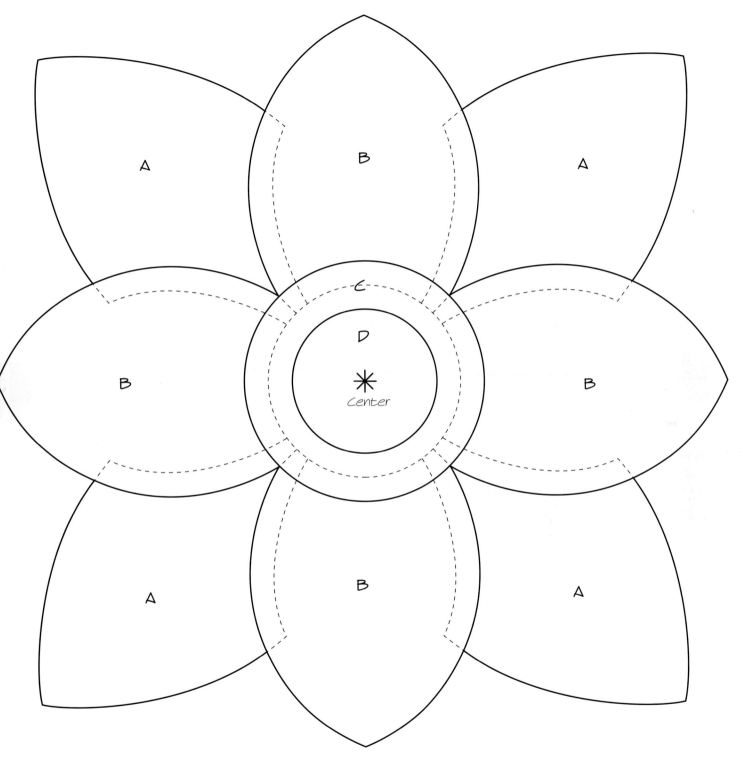

Dahlia Appliqué Pattern and Placement Guide

NINE-PATCH AND RAILS

Set on the diagonal, alternating Nine-Patch and Rail Fence blocks create this quilt's design in graphic black and white. Strip piecing makes the patchwork fast, easy, and fun. Signatures from well-wishers make this friendship quilt an affair to remember.

MATERIALS
for finished size 74" x 91"*

For 52 Nine-Patch blocks
   and 71 Rail Fence blocks:
57 (2½" x 21") black strips

For blocks and borders:
2¾ yards white fabric
2⅛ yards black print fabric
½ yard white print fabric

1 yard binding fabric
   (optional)
5½ yards backing fabric or
   2¾ yards 90"-wide muslin
81" x 96" precut batting

This quilt fits a twin or double bed. Requirements for other sizes are listed on page 118.

CUTTING
Cut all strips cross-grain unless stated otherwise.

From white fabric, cut:
• 75 (2½" x 21") strips.

From white print fabric, cut:
• 7 (2¼"-wide) strips for inner border.

From black print fabric, cut:
• 2 (4¼" x 75") lengthwise strips and 2 (4¼" x 65") lengthwise strips for middle border.
• 6 (9¼") squares. Cut each square in quarters diagonally to get a total of 24 setting triangles.
• 2 (5⅛") squares. Cut each square in half diagonally to get a total of 4 corner triangles.
• 11 (2½" x 21") strips. From these, cut 32 (2½" x 6½") strips for outer border.

MAKING BLOCKS
Finished size of blocks is 6" square.
1. For Strip Set 1, select 1 black strip and 2 white strips. Join white strips to both sides of black strip (*Strip Set 1 Diagram*). Make 31 of Strip Set 1. Press seam allowances toward black fabrics. Set aside 7 strip sets for Nine-Patch blocks. From remainder, cut each strip set into 6½"-wide segments as shown to get a total of 71 completed Rail Fence blocks, 35 for diagonal set and 36 for outer border.

2. For Strip Set 2, select 1 white strip and 2 black strips. Join black strips to both sides of white strip (*Strip Set 2 Diagram*). Make 13 of Strip Set 2. Press seam allowances toward black fabrics. Cut each strip set into 2½"-wide segments to get a total of 104 segments. Cut 7 reserved Strip Set 1s in same manner to get 52 (2½"-wide) segments for Nine-Patch blocks.

3. Join 2 segments from Strip Set 2 to both sides of 1 Strip Set 1 segment to complete 1 block (*Nine-Patch Block Assembly Diagram*).

4. Make 52 Nine-Patch blocks. Square up blocks to 6½" x 6½".

(Continued)

Strip Set 1 Diagram—Make 31.

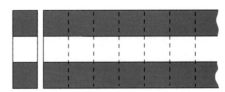

Strip Set 2 Diagram—Make 13.

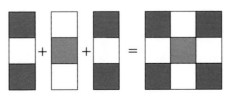

Nine-Patch Block Assembly Diagram

JOINING BLOCKS

This quilt is an example of a diagonal set with alternating blocks. The Nine-Patch blocks are set 6 x 8.

1. Lay out blocks and setting triangles in 13 diagonal rows (Quilt Assembly Diagram), alternating Nine-Patch blocks and Rail Fence blocks as shown. First and last blocks in each row are always Nine-Patches. Note how Rail Fence blocks are turned from row to row. Set aside 4 Nine-Patch blocks and 36 Rail Fence blocks for outer border.

2. When satisfied with placement, join blocks in each row. Press seam allowances toward Rail Fence blocks. Referring to photo, join rows.

ADDING BORDERS

1. Join 2 white print strips for each inner side border. Referring to instructions on page 150, measure quilt from top to bottom; then trim borders to match length. Join borders to quilt sides. Press seam allowances toward borders.

2. Cut 1 remaining white print strip in half; then join 1½ strips for top border. Measure quilt from side to side and trim border to match width. Join to quilt top. Repeat for bottom border. Press seam allowances toward borders.

3. For middle border, measure length of quilt and trim longer black print strips to fit; join borders to quilt. Measure and sew top and bottom borders in same manner.

4. For side border, select 10 Rail Fence blocks and 9 (6½"-long) strips of black print fabric. Referring to photo, join blocks in a row, sewing 1 black strip between each pair of blocks. Join border to quilt side, easing as necessary. Repeat for opposite side border.

5. For top border, join 8 blocks and 7 extra strips in same manner. Sew a Nine-Patch block to each end of strip as shown. Join border to top edge, easing as necessary. Repeat for bottom border.

Quilt Assembly Diagram

VARIABLE SIZES

Size	Wall/Crib	Queen	King
Finished Size	48½" x 57"	82½" x 91"	100" x 100"
Number of Blocks			
Nine-Patch	12	56	81
Rail Fence	6	42	64
Blocks Set	3 x 4	7 x 8	9 x 9
Setting Triangles	10	26	32
Border Widths (finished size)	1¾", 3¾", 6"	1¾", 3¾", 6"	1¾", 3¾", 6"

Finishing

1. Divide backing fabric into 2 (2¾-yard) lengths. Cut 1 piece in half length-wise. Sew a narrow panel to each side of wide panel. Press seam allowances toward narrow panels.

2. Mark desired quilting designs on quilt top. Quilt shown is outline-quilted.

3. Layer backing, batting, and quilt top. Baste. Quilt as desired.

4. Use remaining scraps to make 9½ yards of straight-grain binding, or make binding from a single fabric. See pages 158 and 159 for instructions on making and applying binding.

Quilt by Diane Tatreau of Omaha, Nebraska

CANDY WRAPPERS

Traditional appliquéd fans and speedy diagonal corners combine
to produce a delightful motif that looks like gaily wrapped little packages,
spools, or colorful candy treats. Whatever it looks like to you, this party favor
dances across the quilt looking equally charming on a light or a dark background.

MATERIALS

for finished size 66" x 81"*

For 80 blocks:
70 (7" x 10") scraps for fan blades
40 (8") squares for "candy" centers
4½ yards white fabric (includes binding)

For borders:
1 yard green check fabric

5 yards backing fabric or 2⅛ yards 90"-wide muslin
72" x 90" precut batting

* *This quilt fits a twin bed. Requirements for other sizes are listed below.*

CUTTING

Make templates for patterns A and B on page 122. Refer to page 144 for tips on making templates.
    Cut all strips cross-grain.

From *each* 7" x 10" scrap, cut:
• 8 of Template A to get a total of 560 fan blades.

From *each* 8" square, cut:
• 2 of Template B to get a total of 80 fan bases.
• 2 (3") squares for diagonal corners.

From white fabric, cut:
• 1 (30") square for bias binding or 8 (2½"-wide) strips for straight-grain binding.
• 80 (8") squares.

From green check fabric, cut:
• 8 (3½"-wide) strips for border.

MAKING BLOCKS

Finished size of block is 7½" square.
1. Select 7 A blades for each fan. Join blades side by side (Diagram A). Press seam allowances to 1 side. Turn under edge at top curve and press or baste.
2. Pin each fan on a white square,

aligning outside raw edges of fan with sides of square.
3. Select 1 B fan base for each block. Turn seam allowance under on curved edge and baste. Pin B piece at corner of white square, aligning raw edges at sides (Diagram B). Basted curve of B piece should cover ¼" at bottom of fan blades.
4. Appliqué curved edge of B piece to bottom of fan blades. Then appliqué top curve of fan to background square.
5. Turn each appliquéd block over to wrong side. Trim white fabric behind fan and base, leaving a ¼" seam allowance.

(Continued)

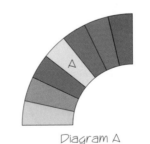

Diagram A

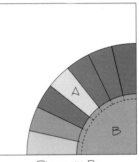

Diagram B

VARIABLE SIZES

Size	Wall/Crib	Double	Queen/King
Finished Size	36" x 51"	81" x 96"	96" x 96"
Number of Blocks	24	120	144
Blocks Set	4 x 6	10 x 12	12 x 12
Border Width (finished size)	3"	3"	3"

6. This design depends on fabrics matching in connecting corners, so it's a good idea to lay out blocks in rows before sewing diagonal corners. Select 8 blocks for Row 1. Position first block with fan in lower right corner (*Row Assembly Diagram*). Position second block with fan in upper right corner. Alternate positions of remaining blocks across row as shown. For Row 2, select 4 blocks with B pieces that match Bs at bottom edge of Row 1 and position these as shown. Then fill in Row 2 with 4 more blocks. Continue laying out rows in this manner, alternating rows 1 and 2. Move blocks around to achieve a balance of color and value.

7. When satisfied with placement of blocks, pin a 3" square of appropriate scrap fabric to corner of each block.

8. See page 17 for instructions on sewing diagonal corners. Stitch diagonal corners on corner of each block opposite fan.

9. Make 80 blocks with diagonal corners. Square up blocks to 8" x 8".

Joining Blocks

This quilt is an example of a straight set, with the blocks set 8 x 10. See setting illustration on page 149.

1. Return completed blocks to your layout of 10 horizontal rows of 8 blocks each (*Row Assembly Diagram*). Check to be sure fabrics match at corners where blocks meet. When satisfied with placement, join blocks in each row.

2. Join rows, alternating rows 1 and 2 as shown in photo.

Adding Borders

1. Join 2 (3½"-wide) border strips end-to-end to make 1 border for each side of quilt.

2. Referring to instructions on page 150, measure quilt. Trim 2 borders to match length. Join borders to quilt sides.

3. Measure quilt width and trim 2 borders to match. Join borders to quilt top and bottom. Press seam allowances toward borders.

Row 1—Make 5.

Row 2—Make 5.

Row Assembly Diagram

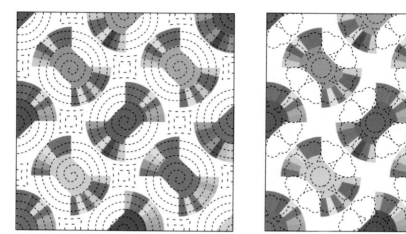

Alternate Quilting Diagrams

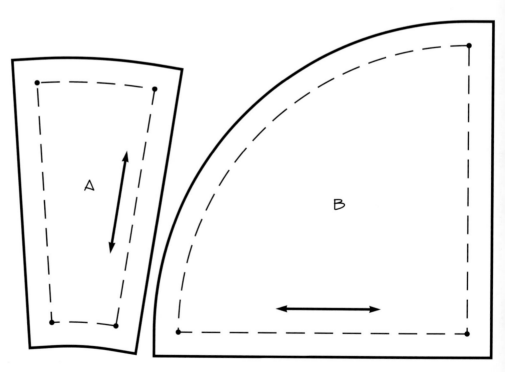

A

B

FINISHING

1. Divide backing fabric into 2 (2½-yard) lengths. Cut 1 piece in half lengthwise. Sew a narrow panel to each side of wide panel. Press seam allowances toward narrow panels.

2. On quilt shown, diagonal lines of quilting start in top left corner and continue across surface of quilt, spaced 1" apart. Two alternative quilting ideas are shown here (Alternate Quilting Diagrams). Mark desired quilting designs on quilt top.

3. Layer backing, batting, and quilt top. Baste. Quilt as desired.

4. Make 8½ yards of bias or straight-grain binding. See pages 158 and 159 for instructions on making and applying binding.

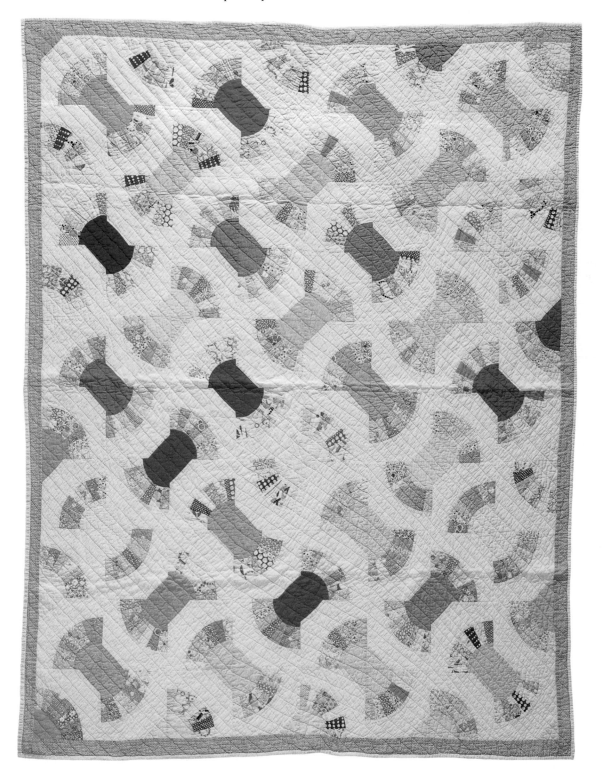

DRESDEN PLATE

Trade scraps with friends to get lots of fabrics for this sunny quilt.
Turn blade points with a quick seam. Joined in a circle, blades are
appliquéd to a background square. Other names for this design
include Texas Sunflower and Calico Rose.

MATERIALS
for finished size 87" x 100"*

For 184 blocks:
552 (5") squares of scraps
¾ yard green fabric

For blocks, border, and
    binding:
4½ yards muslin

8¼ yards backing fabric or
    2¾ yards 108"-wide
    muslin
120" x 120" precut batting

*This quilt fits a double or queen
bed. Requirements for other sizes
are listed on page 127.

CUTTING
Directions on making templates are on
page 144. Make a patchwork template
for Pattern X on page 126 and an appliqué template for Pattern Y. Add seam
allowance when cutting Y pieces from
fabric.

Cut all strips cross-grain unless stated
otherwise.

From each 5" square, cut:
• 4 (2¼" x 2½") strips for plate blades,
  to get a total of 2,208 (12 for each
  block).

From green fabric, cut:
• 184 of Pattern Y.

From muslin, cut:
• 4 (6¾" x 67") lengthwise strips for
  inner border.
• 1 (34") square for continuous bias
  binding or 10 (2½"-wide) strips for
  straight-grain binding.
• 184 (6¾") squares.

MAKING BLOCKS
Finished size of block is 6¼" square.
1. With right sides facing, fold each
blade strip in half lengthwise to measure
1⅛" x 2½". Machine-stitch across 1
short end of each folded segment.
Chain-piece all blades before going to
next step (Diagram A).
2. Trim sewn corners (Diagram B).
3. Turn clipped corners right side out
(Diagram C). Carefully insert seam rip-
per in tips to push out sharp points.
Press points flat.
4. Place X template on wrong side,
aligning corners of template and blade
(Diagram D). With pencil, trace template
at sides and bottom. Trim blades on
marked lines.
5. Select 12 blades for each block. Join
blades in groups of 3 (Block Assembly
Diagram). Check each quarter-plate
against full-size pattern on page 126 to
be sure seams are accurate. Join 2 quar-
ter-plates to make a half; then join
halves. Press seam allowances. *Note:*
Quilt shown has 13 blades in each plate.
For ease of construction, this pattern is
for a 12-blade plate.
6. Fold each muslin square in half vertically and horizontally, finger-pressing
creases for placement guides. Pin 1 plate
on each square, aligning seams with
placement guides. Baste inside curve of
plate in place; then appliqué ends of
blades.
7. Prepare Y centers for appliqué.
Directions on preparing pieces for hand
appliqué are on page 147. Appliqué Y
over center of plate. Complete appliqué
for 184 blocks. (Continued)

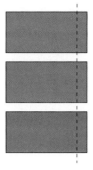

Diagram A

Trim.

Fold

Diagram B

Diagram C

Template

Diagram D

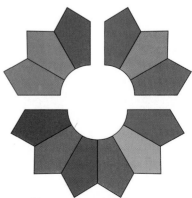

Block Assembly Diagram

Joining Blocks

The interior of this quilt is an example of a straight set, with blocks set 8 x 10. See setting illustration on page 149.

1. Lay out 80 blocks in 10 horizontal rows, with 8 blocks in each row (Row Assembly Diagram). When satisfied with placement, join blocks in each row. Press seam allowances in opposite directions from row to row.

2. Join rows to complete center section.

Adding Borders

1. Referring to instructions on page 150, measure length of center section; then trim 2 muslin border strips to match length. Join 1 strip to each side of quilt. Press seam allowances toward borders.

2. Measure width of quilt; then trim 2 muslin border strips to match width. Join 1 strip each to top and bottom of quilt.

3. For 1 side border, lay out 2 vertical rows with 12 blocks in each row. Referring to photo, join blocks in pairs; then join pairs to assemble border. Join border to 1 side of quilt, easing as necessary. Repeat for opposite side border.

4. For top border, lay out 2 horizontal rows with 14 blocks in each row. Join blocks in pairs; then join pairs to assemble border. Join border to top edge of quilt, easing as necessary. Repeat for bottom border.

Finishing

1. Divide backing fabric into 3 (2¾-yard) lengths. Cut 1 piece in half lengthwise. Discard 1 narrow panel. Sew wide panels to sides of remaining narrow panel. Press seam allowances toward wide panels.

2. On quilt shown, plates are outline-quilted and a 2"-square diamond is quilted at intersection of 4 blocks. A cable is quilted in muslin border. Mark desired quilting designs on quilt top.

3. Layer backing, batting, and quilt top. Backing seams will parallel top and bottom edges of quilt. Baste. Quilt as desired.

4. Make 10¾ yards of bias or straight-grain binding. See pages 158 and 159 for instructions on making and applying binding.

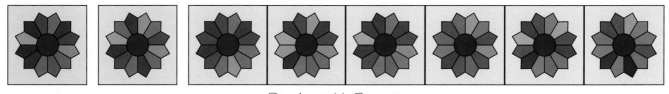

Row Assembly Diagram

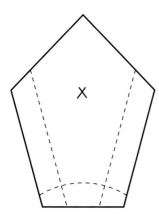

X

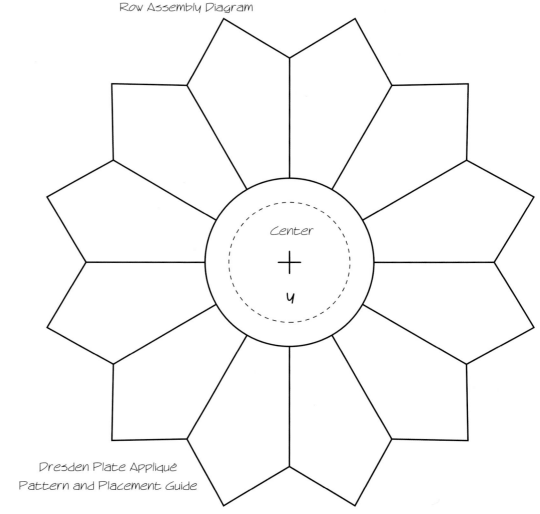

Center

+

4

Dresden Plate Appliqué
Pattern and Placement Guide

Quilt by Dorothy Schrock Shank of Sterling, Illinois

VARIABLE SIZES

Size	Wall/Crib	Twin	King
Finished Size	44" x 50"	69" x 87½"	100" x 100"
Number of Blocks	56	124	212
Blocks Set (center section)	7 x 8	5 x 8	10 x 10
Inner Border Width (finished size)	none	6¼"	6¼"
Border Blocks Set	none	11 x 10	16 x 12

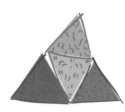

1000 PYRAMIDS

This all-over design is assembled in rows, not block units
like most other quilts. Make it randomly scrappy, or group triangles
by value or color to create patterns within the design.

CUTTING

Cut all strips cross-grain.

Instructions are given for either rotary cutting or cutting with templates. Patterns for triangles X and Y are on page 130.

From 4¼" x 5" scraps, cut:

• 1,040 of Template X.

If you prefer to cut without using a template, see *Diagram A* for cutting measurements. (An alternate suggestion is shown if you're cutting 2 triangles from a larger scrap.)

From 2¾" x 4¾" scraps, cut:

• 26 of Template Y and 26 of Template Y reversed. If you prefer to cut without using a template, see *Diagram B* for cutting measurements.

From black fabric, cut:

• 10 (3½"-wide) strips for border.

From burgundy fabric, cut:

• 1 (34") square for bias binding or 10 (2½"-wide) strips for straight-grain binding.

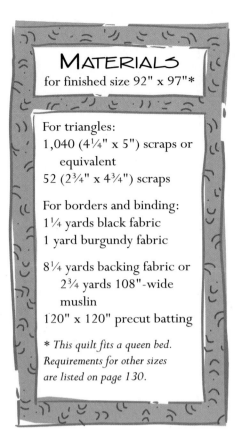

MATERIALS
for finished size 92" x 97"*

For triangles:
1,040 (4¼" x 5") scraps or equivalent
52 (2¾" x 4¾") scraps

For borders and binding:
1¼ yards black fabric
1 yard burgundy fabric

8¼ yards backing fabric or 2¾ yards 108"-wide muslin
120" x 120" precut batting

This quilt fits a queen bed. Requirements for other sizes are listed on page 130.

QUILT TOP ASSEMBLY

This quilt is an exception to the block-by-block assembly of most traditional quilts. Triangles are simply joined in horizontal rows; then rows are joined to complete the quilt top.

1. For Row 1, join 40 X triangles in a row (*Row Assembly Diagram*). Add 1 Y triangle at each end of row. For Row 2, join 40 X triangles as shown. Add 1 Y rev. triangle at each end of row. Make 13 each of rows 1 and 2.

2. Lay out rows, alternating rows as shown in photo. Join rows.

ADDING BORDERS

1. Join 2 black strips for top border. Referring to instructions on page 150, measure quilt; then trim borders to match width. Join borders to top edge of quilt. Repeat for bottom border.

2. Join 3 black strips for each side border. Measure quilt as before; then trim border to match quilt length. Join borders to quilt sides. Press seam allowances toward borders. (Continued)

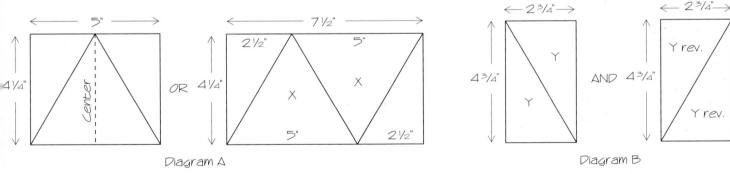

Diagram A

Diagram B

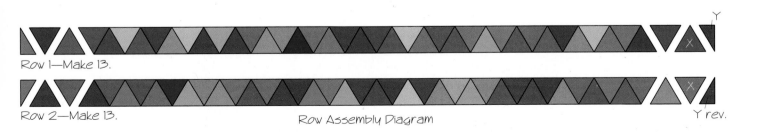

Row 1—Make 13.

Row 2—Make 13.

Row Assembly Diagram

FINISHING

1. Divide backing fabric into 3 (2¾-yard) lengths. Cut 1 piece in half lengthwise; discard 1 narrow panel. Sew a wide panel to each side of narrow panel. Press seam allowances toward wide panels.

2. On quilt shown, triangles are outline-quilted and a 2"-wide cable is quilted in the border. Two alternative quilting designs are shown here (Alternate Quilting Diagrams). Mark desired quilting designs on quilt top.

3. Layer backing, batting, and quilt top. (Backing seams will parallel top and bottom edges, not sides.) Baste. Quilt as desired.

4. Make 11 yards of bias or straight-grain binding. See pages 158 and 159 for instructions on making and applying binding.

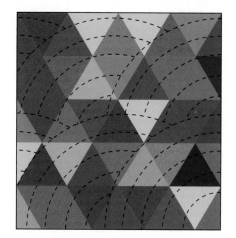

Alternate Quilting Diagrams

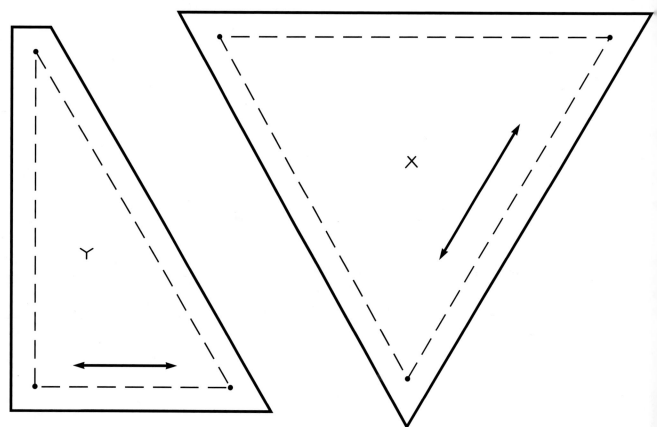

VARIABLE SIZES

Size	Wall/Crib	Twin	King
Finished Size	42⅝" x 43½"	65" x 86½"	96" x 101"
Number of Rows	11	23	26
X Triangles Per Row	17	27	40
Border Width (finished size)	2½"	3"	5"

Y

X

Quilt by Paula Vines of Mountain Home, Arkansas

We loved the quilt on this pretty antique bed. We turned the quilt sideways to make them compatible, which goes to show that creative solutions present themselves at every turn.

PANSIES IN THE WINDOW

This quilt combines a pretty appliquéd pansy with a traditional block called Attic Windows. Hand embroidery stitches add detail to a garden of flowers made from solid-colored fabrics.

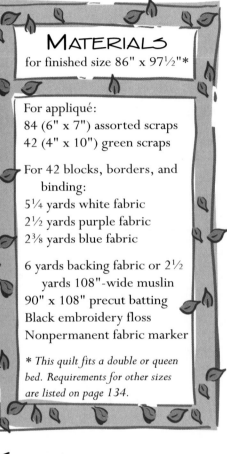

MATERIALS

for finished size 86" x 97½"*

For appliqué:
84 (6" x 7") assorted scraps
42 (4" x 10") green scraps

For 42 blocks, borders, and binding:
5¼ yards white fabric
2½ yards purple fabric
2⅜ yards blue fabric

6 yards backing fabric or 2½ yards 108"-wide muslin
90" x 108" precut batting
Black embroidery floss
Nonpermanent fabric marker

This quilt fits a double or queen bed. Requirements for other sizes are listed on page 134.

CUTTING

Before cutting, choose an appliqué technique. Directions on cutting pieces for hand appliqué are on page 144. Make templates for patterns A–F on page 135. Add seam allowance when cutting fabric.

Cut all strips cross-grain unless stated otherwise.

From 6" x 7" scraps, cut:
• 42 B petals.
• 42 C petals.
• 42 D petals.
• 42 E petals.
• 42 F petals.

From *each* green fabric, cut:
• 3 A leaves.

From white fabric, cut:
• 2 (8½" x 104") lengthwise strips and 2 (8½" x 92") lengthwise strips for outer borders.
• 42 (9") squares.

From blue fabric, cut:
• 1 (3¼" x 84") lengthwise strip for inner border.
• 42 (3¼" x 12") strips for blocks.

From purple fabric, cut:
• 1 (3¼" x 75") lengthwise strip for inner border.
• 1 (32") square for bias binding or 9 (2½"-wide) strips for straight-grain binding.
• 42 (3¼" x 12") strips for blocks.

MAKING BLOCKS

Finished size of block is 11¼" square.

1. For each block, select 3 A leaves, 1 B and 1 C petal of the same fabric, and 1 each of D, E, and F petals of the same fabric. Lightly trace embroidery details on D, E, and F. Prepare leaves and petals for appliqué. Directions on preparing pieces for hand appliqué are on page 147.

2. Fold each white square in half diagonally, vertically, and horizontally, finger-pressing a crease in each direction for placement guides. Position square over printed pansy pattern, matching center of square with marked center of pattern. Lightly trace outline of pattern onto square.

3. Position A leaves on square and appliqué.

4. When leaves are appliquéd, position B petal and appliqué.

5. Continue to place and appliqué petals in alphabetical order. Complete appliqué for 42 blocks.

6. Referring to pattern, use 2 strands of floss to work embroidery details as shown. Embroidery stitch diagrams are on page 135.

7. See page 151 for tips on sewing a mitered corner. Join a 12" blue strip to left side of each block and a purple strip to bottom of block. Press seam allowances toward colored strips (Miter Diagram); then miter corners. Press seam allowances open.

8. Square up blocks to 11¾" x 11¾".

(Continued)

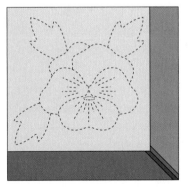

Miter Diagram

Joining Blocks

This quilt is an example of a straight set, with the blocks set 6 x 7. See setting illustration on page 149.

1. Lay out blocks in 7 horizontal rows, with 6 blocks in each row (*Row Assembly Diagram*). When satisfied with placement, join blocks in each row.

2. Join rows as shown in photo.

Adding Borders

1. Referring to instructions on page 150, measure length of quilt; then trim blue border to match length. Join border to right side of quilt. Press seam allowance toward border.

2. Measure width of quilt; then trim purple border to match width. Join border to top edge of quilt. Press seam allowances toward borders.

3. Read instructions for mitered borders on pages 150 and 151. Measure length of quilt and mark both 104"-long borders to match length. Measure width of quilt and mark 1 remaining border to match width. Join longer borders to quilt sides; then add remaining marked border to bottom edge. Miter corners.

4. Measure width of quilt and trim remaining border strip accordingly. Join border to top edge, sewing straight (butted) corners.

Finishing

1. Divide backing fabric into 2 (3-yard) lengths. Cut 1 piece in half lengthwise. Sew a narrow panel to each side of wide panel. Press seam allowances toward narrow panels.

2. On quilt shown, pansies are outline-quilted and a spiral design is quilted in the outer border. Mark desired quilting designs on quilt top.

3. Layer backing, batting, and quilt top. Baste. Quilt as desired.

4. Make 10½ yards of bias or straight-grain binding. See pages 158 and 159 for instructions on making and applying binding.

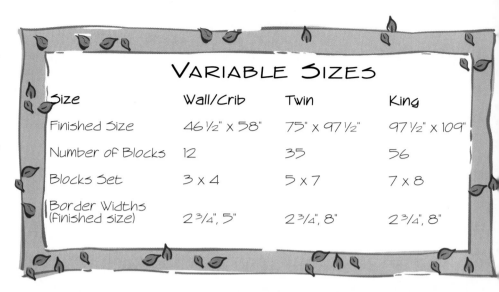

VARIABLE SIZES

Size	Wall/Crib	Twin	King
Finished Size	46 ½" x 58"	75" x 97 ½"	97 ½" x 109"
Number of Blocks	12	35	56
Blocks Set	3 x 4	5 x 7	7 x 8
Border Widths (finished size)	2 ¾", 5"	2 ¾", 8"	2 ¾", 8"

Row Assembly Diagram

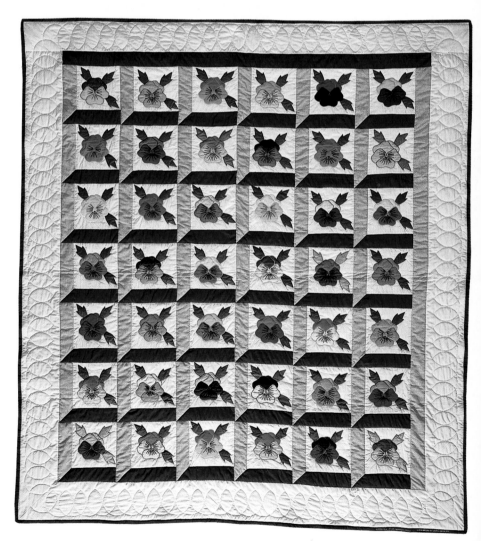

Quilt by Laurel Warner Larsen of Cloverdale, California

Center

Satin
Stitch

Outline
Stitch

Pansies Applique Pattern and Placement Guide

Satin Stitch

Outline Stitch

LADDER TO THE STARS

Value—placement of light and dark—is key to these Ladder blocks.
Turning the blocks correctly causes the patchwork elements
to form a chain that is surrounded by a border of plaid Star blocks.

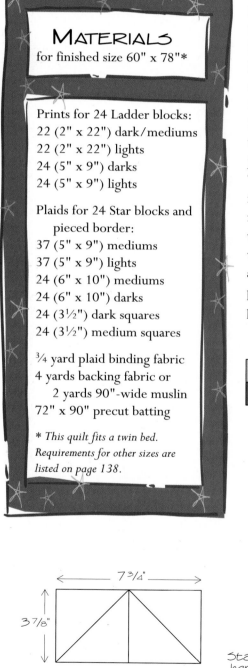

MATERIALS
for finished size 60" x 78"*

Prints for 24 Ladder blocks:
22 (2" x 22") dark/mediums
22 (2" x 22") lights
24 (5" x 9") darks
24 (5" x 9") lights

Plaids for 24 Star blocks and
    pieced border:
37 (5" x 9") mediums
37 (5" x 9") lights
24 (6" x 10") mediums
24 (6" x 10") darks
24 (3½") dark squares
24 (3½") medium squares

¾ yard plaid binding fabric
4 yards backing fabric or
    2 yards 90"-wide muslin
72" x 90" precut batting

*This quilt fits a twin bed.
Requirements for other sizes are
listed on page 138.*

MAKING LADDER BLOCKS

Finished size of block is 9" square.

1. Join each dark 2" x 22" strip to a light strip (Diagram A). Press seam allowances toward dark fabrics. Make 22 strip sets. From these, rotary-cut 240 (2"-wide) segments.

2. Select 2 segments at random and join to make a four-patch (Diagram B). To randomize selection, put segments in a pillowcase—shake them up, and reach in blind to select each pair. (Vow to join any 2 you pull out, no matter what, or else you'll start to worry about coordinating.) Make 120 four-patches, 5 for each block. Each four-patch should be 3½" square.

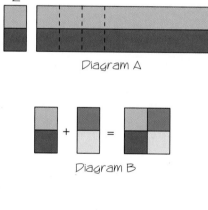

2"

Diagram A

+ =

Diagram B

3. On *wrong* side of 1 light 5" x 9" print scrap, draw 2 (3⅞") squares (Diagram C), leaving a small margin on all sides of drawing. Then draw a diagonal line through each square as shown. With right sides facing, match light scrap with 1 dark scrap.

4. Stitch ¼" seam on both sides of diagonal lines, pivoting at corners to sew continuously from start to finish (Diagram D). Press. Cut on all drawn lines to get 4 triangle-squares. Make 96 triangle-squares, 4 for each block. Each triangle square should be 3½" square. Press seam allowances toward dark fabric.

5. Select 4 triangle-squares and 5 four-patches for each block. (Don't give in to that temptation to coordinate!) Arrange units in 3 horizontal rows (Ladder Block Assembly Diagram). Join units in each row; then join rows to complete block.

6. Make 24 Ladder blocks. Square up blocks to 9½" x 9½". (Continued)

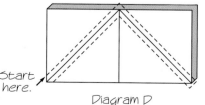

7¾"

3⅞"

Diagram C

Start here.

Diagram D

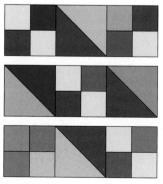

Ladder Block Assembly Diagram

MAKING STAR BLOCKS

Finished size of block is 9" square.

1. Follow steps 3 and 4 on page 136 to make 148 triangle-squares from 5" x 9" pieces of light and medium plaid. (This includes 52 for outer border.)

2. To make hourglass (4-triangle) units, begin by making triangle-squares in nearly the same manner; with a few more steps, you'll turn 4 triangle-squares into 4 hourglass units. Select 1 medium/dark pair of 6" x 10" scraps. This time, draw 2 (4¼") squares (Diagram E); then proceed to make 4 triangle-squares as before.

3. On wrong side of 1 (4¼") triangle-square, draw a diagonal line that bisects the seam (Diagram F). With contrasting fabrics facing, match this square with another triangle-square, aligning seams. Stitch ¼" seam on both sides of drawn line, sewing through both triangle-squares. Cut units apart on drawn line to get 2 identical hourglass units. Repeat with remaining pair of triangle-squares to get 2 more units. Make 96 hourglass units, 4 for each star block. Each unit should be 3½" square.

4. Select 4 triangle-squares, 4 hour-glass units, and 1 (3½") square of dark plaid for each block. Arrange units in 3 horizontal rows (Star Block Assembly Diagram). Join units in each row; then join rows to complete block.

5. Make 24 Star blocks. Square up blocks to 9½" x 9½".

MAKING BORDER UNITS

1. For each border unit, join 2 triangle-squares to opposite sides of 1 light plaid square (Diagram G). Make 28 border units. Press seam allowances toward plaid square.

2. Set aside 4 remaining triangle-squares for quilt corners.

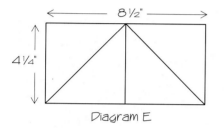

Diagram E

Diagram F

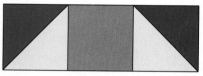

Diagram G

Star Block Assembly Diagram

VARIABLE SIZES

Size	Wall/Crib	Double/Queen	King
Finished Size	60" x 60"	78" x 96"	96" x 96"
Number of Blocks			
Ladder	4	48	64
Star	12	32	36
Blocks Set	4 x 4	8 x 10	10 x 10

JOINING BLOCKS

This quilt is an example of a straight set. The Ladder blocks are set 4 x 6 and surrounded by a border of Star blocks. See illustration of a straight set on page 149.

1. For Row 1, lay out 6 border units in a row with a corner unit at each end (Row Assembly Diagram). For Row 2, lay out a row of 6 star blocks, adding 1 border unit at each end of row. For Row 3, lay out 4 Ladder blocks, turning them as shown; then add star blocks and border units at each end of row. Lay out blocks for rows 4 and 5 in same manner. (Diagram shows half of quilt. Heavier lines separate blocks.)

2. When satisfied with placement, join blocks in each row. Join rows to complete top half of quilt.

3. Repeat to make bottom half of quilt. Join halves to complete quilt.

FINISHING

1. Divide backing fabric into 2 (2-yard) lengths. Cut 1 piece in half lengthwise. Sew a narrow panel to each side of wide panel. Press seam allowances toward narrow panels.

2. Mark desired quilting designs on quilt top. Quilt shown is outline-quilted.

3. Layer backing, batting, and quilt top. Baste. Quilt as desired.

4. Make 8 yards of 2½"-wide bias or straight-grain binding. See pages 158 and 159 for instructions on making and applying binding.

Row 1
Row 2
Row 3
Row 4
Row 5

Row Assembly Diagram

Quilt by Kitty Sorgen of Newbury Park, California

START TO FINISH
BASIC QUILTMAKING TECHNIQUES

THE MAGIC OF SCRAPS

Scrap quilts really *are* magic. But there's no sleight of hand—it's just that almost *anything* works. You can't go wrong. There are no hard-and-fast rules, so the only mistakes you can make are being too serious and trying to exercise control over what should be a free-spirited creation. It's the lack of control, the randomness, that makes a scrap quilt really captivating.

So relax. Don't agonize over choosing fabrics or try to match them. Believe in the magic and put scraps together willy-nilly. You'll have a terrific scrap quilt made before you can say "abracadabra."

MIX IT UP

Look at *Fabric Frolic* (page 6). You'll see big prints and little prints, bright ones and drab ones, prints and plaids—a terrific jumble of everything. But the combination works! It works because of the simplicity of the block (so you're not adding complex design to the jumble of the fabric), and because a neutral sashing and border ties everything together. Eliminating variation of scale, color, or value would only diminish the overall effect.

Another good example of how anything goes is *1000 Pyramids* (page 128). Its triangles are paisleys, plaids, stripes, and prints of every type—everything from purple polka dots to red plaids and blue stripes.

But a monochromatic look can work as well. *Blueprints* (page 84) and *Starry Night* (page 74) are examples of one-color designs. Many of us have favorite colors and, over time, we'll collect lots of scraps in those colors. If you have a range of dark, medium, and light, as well as a variety of large and small prints, then you've got the makings of a scrap quilt. Stick to one color, or add a complementary color for zing like in *Midnight Stars* (page 51).

NEUTRAL PARTIES

In a riot of color, neutrals play an important role. As you study the quilts in this book, you'll find that many, like *Fabric Frolic,* use a neutral to impose a little order.

Ecru, tan, gray, and black are favorite neutrals. Dark blue and brown are sometimes neutral, too. Used as a background or for sashing and borders, these fabrics provide a subtle unity so all the others can be completely random.

USE UP THOSE UGLIES

Someone once said, "Great fabrics make great quilts." But not-so-great fabrics can make great quilts, too. Scrap quilts use up a lot of "uglies"—outdated calicos left over from the seventies or a bargain that was too good to pass up but not pretty enough to use. The odd piece of ugly disappears into the coordinated mayhem that is a scrap quilt. Sometimes it takes a few uglies to really make a scrap quilt work, to fade into the background so that others can stand out.

COTTON CLUB

In scrap quilts, the temptation is great to use bits of old clothing. While this is nice for a trip down memory lane, it can make sewing difficult. Clothing is often made from polyester/cotton blends, and the characteristics that make them ideal for clothes make them inappropriate for quilting.

Blends resist creasing, a desirable trait in a shirt but not for an appliqué that requires a sharp edge. The hard finish that makes polyester so durable also makes quilting difficult.

Cotton remains the best choice for quilts. Add scraps of clothing if nostalgia gets the better of you, but try to use mostly 100% cotton.

BUYING YARDAGE

The fabrics you'll need for each project are shown in the materials list. Yardage is given for sashing, borders, backing, and binding. We allow for narrow widths and shrinkage by estimating yardage based on 42" of usable width. If your fabric is less than 42" wide, you may need more than is listed, even though we allow a little extra for error. If you have a little fabric left over, add it to your scraps!

PREWASHING FABRIC

We recommend that you prewash and press all yardage before you cut it. This helps you to avoid shrinkage and bleeding in your finished quilt. Wash darks and lights separately in the washing machine. Tumble the fabric dry in a warm dryer until slightly damp; then press until dry.

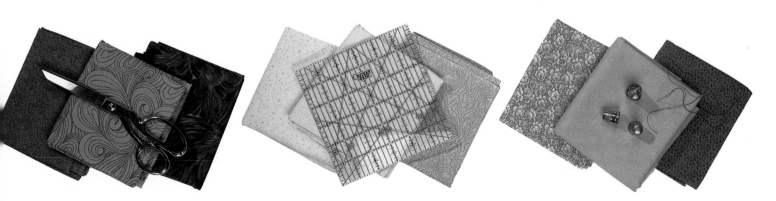

ROTARY CUTTING

Rotary-cut pieces are usually more accurate than pieces marked with templates and cut with scissors. Most of the projects in this book are designed to be rotary cut and therefore have no patterns. Patterns are provided for shapes that do not lend themselves to rotary cutting.

Dimensions given for rotary-cut borders, strips, and pieces always include seam allowances. Unless stated otherwise, cut strips cross-grain (across the width of the fabric, selvage to selvage).

Wash and dry fabric before cutting; then press out all folds and creases. Fabric is often rolled onto bolts offgrain, so it is important to eliminate the center fold.

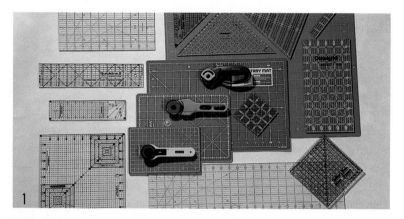

GETTING STARTED

1. Rotary cutters, mats, and rulers come in different sizes and shapes— select ones you find comfortable to use. Change the cutter blade regularly. An 18" x 24" mat is fine for most cutting, but you'll want a smaller mat for cutting scraps. Use acrylic rulers marked in ⅛" increments as well as 45° and 60° angles. The most useful rulers are a 6" x 24" (for borders), a 15" square, a 6" x 12", and a 6" square.

SQUARING UP

2. Before you cut strips, you must trim the fabric so that the raw edge is straight and perpendicular to the selvage. Begin by folding the fabric in half, matching selvages. Fold the fabric in half again, matching selvages to the first fold. By folding the fabric in fourths in this way, cuts will be a manageable 11" long.

3. Align a square ruler with the bottom edge of the fabric, with the left edge of the ruler ½" from the uneven fabric end. Butt a long ruler against the left side of the square. Remove the square, leaving the long ruler in position.

4. Hold the ruler firmly in place, being careful not to shift it. Starting at the bottom of the fabric, roll the cutter along the right edge of the ruler. Exert firm, even pressure on the cutter as it trims the fabric.

CUTTING STRIPS, SQUARES, AND TRIANGLES

5. Straight, accurately cut strips are essential for good patchwork. To cut a strip, position the ruler at the squared-off edge of the fabric. Measure the desired strip width from the edge of the fabric to the ruler's edge.

6. Check frequently to see that cuts remain straight. If a strip is not cut at a true right angle to the fold, it will bow in the center. Square up fabric as often as necessary to produce straight strips.

7. Use a small ruler for small cuts. Align the desired measurement on the ruler with the strip end and cut across the strip.

8. To rotary-cut right-angle triangles, it's usually best to start with a square. When you cut a square in half diagonally, you get two triangles with short legs on the straight of the grain and the hypotenuse (long diagonal edge opposite the right angle) on the bias. Sometimes, however, you want a straight-grain hypotenuse and bias legs. In these cases, the instructions will direct you to cut the square in quarters diagonally to get four triangles—in other words, cut the square in an X. To do this, make the first diagonal cut and then rotate the mat (don't lift the fabric) so that you can align the ruler on the opposite diagonal and cut again.

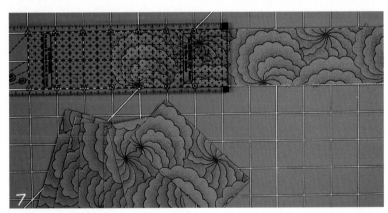

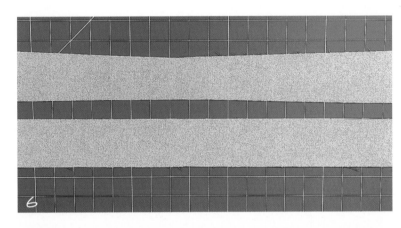

CUTTING WITH TEMPLATES

A template is a duplication of a printed pattern that you use to trace a shape onto fabric. Straight-sided shapes can be rotary-cut, but you need templates to accurately mark curves and other complex shapes. However, some quilters like to use templates for all shapes.

All patterns in this book are full sized. Patchwork patterns show the seam line (dashed) and the cutting line (solid). Patterns for appliqué do not include seam allowances. To check the accuracy of your templates and marking, make a test block before cutting out pieces for more blocks.

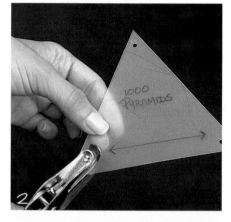

MAKING TEMPLATES

We recommend template plastic, which is easy to cut and can be used repeatedly. Best of all, its transparency allows you to trace a pattern directly onto it.

1. Trace the pattern onto plastic, using a ruler to draw straight lines.

2. If desired, punch ⅛" holes in the template's seam line to enable you to mark pivot points.

3. For patchwork, trace templates *facedown* on *wrong* side of fabric. Use common lines for efficient cutting.

4. For hand appliqué, trace template *faceup* on *right* side of fabric. (The lightly drawn line should disappear into the fold of the appliqué when it is stitched to the background fabric.) Position tracings at least ½" apart so you can add seam allowance when cutting each piece.

5. A window template can serve two purposes. It provides the guidance of a drawn seam line, which is particularly useful for setting in. Marked on the right side of the fabric, a window template also helps you to center specific motifs with accuracy.

PIECING, PRESSING, AND PINNING

The standard seam allowance for patch-work is ¼". If your seams vary, corners and points may not match and your project will be the wrong size.

On many machines, the distance from the needle to the edge of the presser foot is exactly ¼". If you don't have a foot that gauges ¼", buy one that does or mark a seam guide on the throat plate.

To test your seams, cut two 3" squares. With right sides facing and edges aligned, join squares on one side, sewing 14 stitches per inch. Do not backstitch. The combined width of the squares should be 5½". If you get a different measurement, adjust the seam guide as needed.

Use 100% cotton or cotton-covered polyester thread for machine patch-work. A medium gray or tan is often the best color to use with scraps since either one blends with most fabrics.

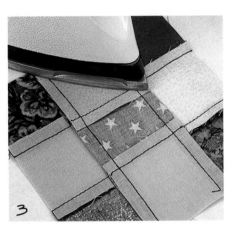

PIECING

1. When you have many units to sew, save time by chain piecing, sewing assembly-line style. As soon as one unit is stitched, feed in the next—the machine stitches on air a few times before the needle strikes the next piece, making a small thread link. Carry the chain to the ironing board and snip the units apart as you press them.

2. When triangular units are joined to other units, the seams cross in an X on the back. Watch for this X as you sew units together—if the joining seam goes through the center of each X, the triangle will have a nice sharp point on the front.

PRESSING

3. Press each seam before stitching across it. With right sides still facing, press the seam to set the stitches. Then open out the fabric, right side up, and press the seam allowances to one side. Press seam allowances in opposite directions from row to row so that they will offset each other when seams meet. If possible, press seam allowances toward the darker fabric. Always *press* rather than iron. Lift the iron to move it, and press with an up-and-down motion. Sliding the iron back and forth can distort fabric.

PINNING

4. Pinning is necessary only for long seams or where seams must align. Use pin matching to align seams. With right sides facing, align opposing seam allowances. On the top piece, push a pin through the seam line ¼" from the raw edge. Then push the pin through the seam of the bottom piece in the same manner and set the pin. The joining seam should cross the point where the pin entered the fabric. For long seams, pin first at both ends, then the center, and then along the length as needed. As you stitch the seam, remove each pin just before the needle reaches it. (If the needle hits a pin, either one could break and send bits of metal flying at you.)

STRIP PIECING

Many quilts are faster and easier to make with strip piecing. Cutting pre-joined units from assembled strips is also often more accurate than traditional piece-by-piece sewing. This method has become a standard in the repertoire of today's leading quiltmakers.

Begin a project by strip-piecing one unit to learn the techniques. Then you will feel comfortable working assembly-line style with your chosen fabrics.

SEWING STRIP SETS

A strip set is made of strips that are sewn together lengthwise in a particular sequence. Strip sets are later cut into segments to use as blocks or portions of blocks.

1. To make a strip set, pair two strips with right sides facing and raw edges aligned. Machine-stitch with a ¼" seam allowance. Add more strips as directed in the project instructions.

2. With wrong side up, just as you've sewn them, press the strips flat to set the seam.

3. Fold the top strip back, revealing the right side of the strip set. Press seam allowances to one side. After pressing, check to be sure there are no folds or tucks along the seam.

CUTTING SEGMENTS

Once the strip set is sewn and pressed, you will cut it into segments that become preassembled patchwork units.

4. Align the horizontal lines on the ruler with the long raw edges and seams of the strip set. Square up the uneven end of the strip set before you cut the first segment. Keeping the ruler lines parallel with the edges and seams of the strip set, measure and cut the desired width segments.

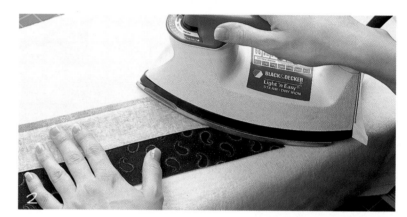

APPLIQUÉ

Appliqué is the process of sewing fabric pieces onto a background fabric. The edges of appliqués are turned under and sewn to the background by hand.

TRADITIONAL APPLIQUÉ

See page 144, Step 4, for tips on making templates and cutting appliqué pieces.

1. Using the drawn line as a guide, turn under and baste the seam allowances on each piece. Do not turn an edge that will be covered by another piece.

2. Pin the appliqué pieces to the background fabric. Using sewing thread that matches the appliqué, make tiny slipstitches to secure the piece. (We used contrasting thread for photography.) Working from right to left, pull the needle through the background fabric and catch a few threads on the fold of the appliqué. Reinsert the needle into the background fabric right next to the last stitch and bring the needle up through the appliqué for the next stitch.

FREEZER-PAPER APPLIQUÉ

Some quilters find it easier to turn edges with this technique, which uses freezer paper as a template.

3. Trace patterns onto the dull side of the freezer paper. Cut out the template on the drawn line. Using a dry iron, press the shiny side of the template to the *wrong* side of the fabric. Leave at least ½" between templates. Cut out each piece, adding ¼" seam allowance. Snip seam allowances at inside curves.

4. Apply fabric glue to the wrong side of the seam allowance. Use your fingers or a cool, dry iron to turn the seam allowance over the template edge.

5. Appliqué pieces as for traditional appliqué. When stitching is complete, cut away the background fabric behind the appliqués, leaving seam allowances. Use tweezers to remove paper pieces.

JOINING BLOCKS

The simplest way to join blocks is in rows, sewing them together in a straight line. All of the quilts in this book are pieced in this manner.

Arrange blocks and setting pieces, if any, on the floor or a large table. Identify the pieces in each row and verify the position of each block. This is play time—moving blocks around to find the best balance of color and value is great fun when making a scrap quilt. Don't start sewing until you're happy with the placement of each block.

As you join the blocks in each row, pick up one block at a time to avoid confusion. Pin-match adjoining seams. (If necessary, re-press a seam to offset seam allowances.) If you find that some blocks are larger than others, pinning may help determine where easing is required. A blast of steam from the iron may help fit the blocks together.

1. When a row is assembled, press seam allowances between blocks in the same direction. For the adjacent row, press seam allowances in the opposite direction.

2. In an alternate set, straight or diagonal, always press seam allowances between blocks toward setting squares or triangles—this creates the least bulk and always results in opposing seam allowances when adjacent rows are joined.

3. Sashing eliminates the need to worry about opposing seam allowances. Assemble horizontal rows with vertical sashing strips between blocks; then press the new seam allowances toward the sashing. If necessary, ease the block to match the length of the sashing strip. Assemble the quilt top with rows of sashing between block rows, always pressing seam allowances toward the sashing strips.

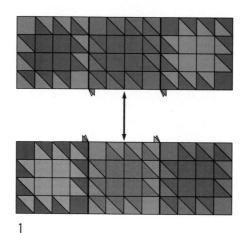

1

2

3

SET VARIATIONS

How blocks are arranged, or set, is an important part of quilt design. The same blocks can look amazingly different in different sets. It's fun to play with blocks to find the most interesting setting.

We used an Anvil block in the illustrations here. In each drawing, darker lines indicate rows for assembly.

STRAIGHT SET

When blocks are joined edge to edge, the patchwork interacts to create new designs where the blocks meet, creating visual effects not present in a single block. A good example is *Kaleidoscope* on page 24.

To assemble a straight set, sew blocks together in rows, either horizontally or vertically as specified. Join rows to complete the quilt top. Matching seam lines at each juncture is important to achieve the best effect.

Most of the quilts in this book are straight sets. Sometimes a design seems complex because adjacent blocks are turned to create different combinations of patchwork (such as *Log Cabin* on page 42), but the assembly is always the same—edge to edge.

ALTERNATE STRAIGHT SET

An alternate straight set is assembled in the same manner as a regular straight set, but two different blocks alternate across the row, checkerboard style.

Sometimes the alternate block is a plain square of a matching or contrasting fabric (see *Button Box,* page 14). This treatment separates blocks and emphasizes the individuality of each block rather than the interaction between them.

In other cases, two different blocks alternate. A good example is *Reunion Star* on page 100. The wonderful illusion of circles is achieved not by complex piecing but by the interaction of alternating blocks.

STRAIGHT SET WITH SASHING

Sashing separates and defines each block, giving a quilt a sense of order. A well-chosen sashing fabric is a unifying element that ties scrappy blocks together.

Sashing can be plain or pieced. Pieced sashing often uses contrasting squares at the intersections where blocks meet. Examples are *Fabric Frolic* on page 6 and *Blueprints* on page 84. Pieced sashing can also be sufficiently complex to blend or interact with the blocks to such a degree that it's hard to tell which parts of the quilt are blocks and which are sashing. An example is *Milky Way* on page 92.

Straight Set

Alternate Straight Set

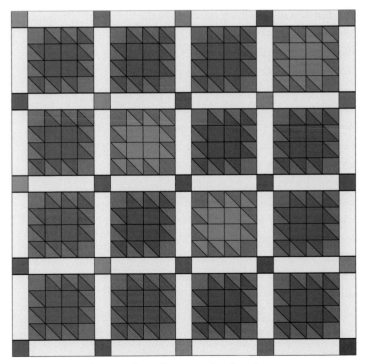

Straight Set with Sashing

Set Variations **149**

BORDERS

Most quilts have one wide border or several narrow ones that frame the central design. Corners can be square or mitered.

In this book, cutting instructions for borders include extra length to allow for variations in piecing. It is necessary to measure your quilt to determine how to trim border strips to fit properly.

MEASURING

It's common for one side of a quilt top to be a slightly different measurement than its opposite side. No matter how careful your piecing, tiny variables add up. If you leave the sides uneven, the finished quilt won't lie flat. You want to sew borders of equal length to opposite sides to square up the quilt.

1. Measure the quilt from top to bottom *through the middle* of the quilt. (For a large quilt, you'll need a 10-foot measuring tape.) Trim both side border strips to this measurement. Sew borders to quilt sides, easing as necessary.

2. For top and bottom borders, measure from side to side through the middle of the quilt. Trim and sew these borders as before.

This example joins side borders first, and then top and bottom borders. Sometimes it is practical to reverse the sequence. Instructions specify the order in which you should sew borders.

SQUARE CORNERS

The type of border shown in steps 1 and 2 is an example of square corners. When top and bottom borders are added, they cross the seam line of the side borders and extend to the edges.

If you want a contrasting corner, measure for top and bottom borders *before* adding side borders. Stitch contrasting squares to the ends of the top and bottom border strips. When sewn to the quilt, the seams of the squares should align with the side border seams.

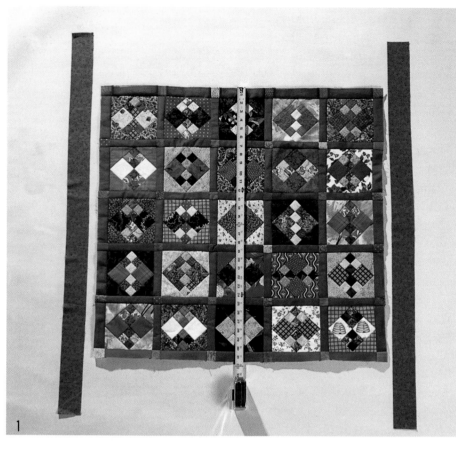

1

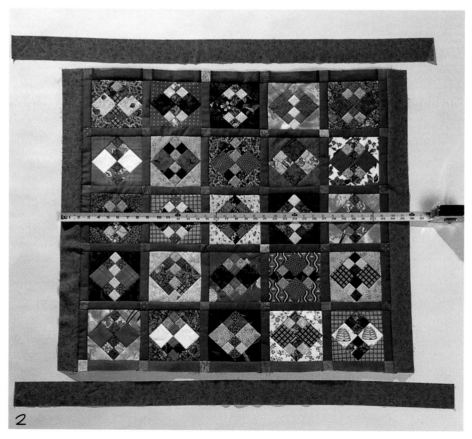

2

MITERED CORNERS

The seam of a mitered corner is more subtle than that of a square corner, so it creates the illusion of a continuous line around the quilt. Mitered corners are particularly suitable for borders of striped fabric or pieced borders.

3. Measure the length and width of the quilt through the middle as described on the opposite page, but do not trim the fabric yet. Mark the center of one side border. Starting at the center, measure along the edge a distance equal to *half* the determined border length. Back up ¼" (seam allowance) and mark. Repeat for the other end of the border. On the wrong side of the quilt, mark the center on all four edges and each corner, ¼" from the edge. Matching marked points, pin the border to the quilt.

4. Backstitching at both ends, sew the border seam from match point to match point. Join remaining border strips in the same manner. (We've used contrasting thread for photography only.)

5. With right sides facing, fold the quilt top diagonally at one corner so adjacent borders are aligned. Pin. Place a ruler with its edge against the fold. Use the ruler's edge as a guide to draw a diagonal line that extends the fold line through the match point to the edge of the border strip.

6. Beginning with a backstitch at the inside corner, stitch on the marked line to the outside edge. Check the right side of the quilt to see that the seam lies flat and any stripes match up as desired. When satisfied with the seam, trim excess fabric from the borders, leaving ¼" seam allowance.

7. Repeat steps 3–5 for remaining corners. At each corner, press seam allowances so that the interior portion of the quilt lies flat. Mitered corner seam allowances can be pressed to one side or open, as you prefer. Then press the seam on the right side of the quilt.

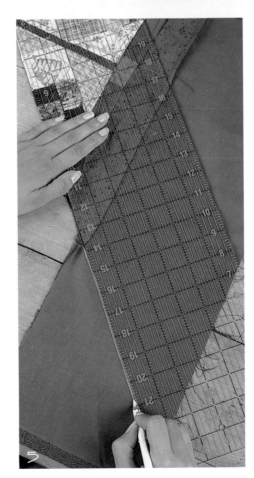

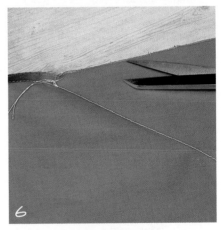

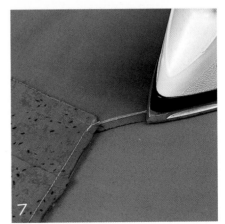

Choosing a Quilting Design

Your work is not finished until the top is sewn to the batting and backing with quilting—running stitches that join the layers, forming subtle patterns that enhance the overall design.

The quilting design is an integral part of a quilt, so choose it with care. Consider these points before making a decision.

• What is your skill level? Simple, straight lines are easiest for beginners.

• How much time do you want to spend? The more quilting, the more time it will take.

• How will the quilt be used? Fancy quilting may not make sense on a quilt that's going to college with a teenager.

• Where will a quilting design show up best? Borders or alternating unpieced blocks are good spots to display a pretty quilting design.

• What fabrics are in the quilt? If you're using a matching thread color, quilting shows more on light fabrics than on dark ones and on solid fabrics more than prints. A complex design quilted on dark, busy print fabrics won't be very visible.

• Can you use a quilting design to add meaning? If the quilt is a wedding gift, for example, quilted motifs such as hearts and lover's knots are nice. Quilted sports motifs, pets, and other images can also enhance your quilt.

Outline and Echo Quilting

The simplest quilting follows the lines of the patchwork or appliqué, often without marking the quilt ahead of time.

Outline quilting is stitched ¼" from the seam lines, just past the extra thickness of the pressed seam allowances. Many quilters use ¼"-wide masking tape as a stitching guide. Used in small segments and removed as you quilt, masking tape leaves no residue on the fabric. Outline

quilting is used to good effect in *Star Path* (page 108) to emphasize the stars.

Quilting in-the-ditch also follows the seam, but the quilting is so close to the seam that it nearly disappears when you release the quilt from the tension of a hoop or frame. This simple quilting style is ideal for machine quilting. On appliquéd quilts, in-the-ditch quilting is stitched closely around the edge of the design, which raises it slightly from the quilt surface.

Echo quilting refers to multiple lines of quilting that follow the outline of an appliqué so the quilting repeats, or echoes, the shape. *Butterflies* (page 28) is a nice example.

Lining Up

Straight line quilting complements patchwork by directing the eye to selected aspects of the design.

In quilts such as *Irish Chain* (page 96), for example, diagonal lines of quilting reinforce the illusion of continuous chains formed by the joined blocks. In *1000 Pyramids* (page 128), quilting lines could define diamond shapes or diagonals to suggest secondary designs in the patchwork.

Some quilters like to contrast geometric patchwork with rounded lines of quilting. Look at *Starry Night* (page 74) for an example—the curved lines of quilting add motion to the design.

Outline Quilting

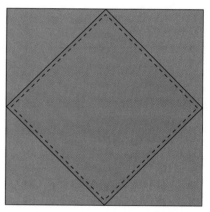

Quilting In-the-Ditch

Echo Quilting

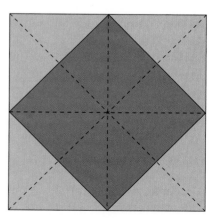

Straight Line Quilting

BACKGROUND FILLERS

Some quilts have background designs quilted in open spaces. Most fillers are patterns of lines stitched vertically, horizontally, or diagonally. Crossing lines make grids of squares or diamonds called cross-hatching. These fillers are easy to mark using only a marker and a ruler. *Kansas Troubles* (page 104) shows an effective use of background quilting. The grid of squares stitched in each large triangle complements the angles of the patchwork.

Not all background fillers are straight lines. Some filler patterns ignore the natural boundaries of the patchwork and create an allover design. Popular fillers of this type are clamshells, concentric circles, and half-circles.

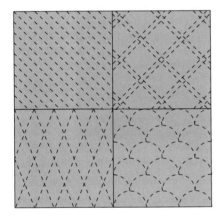

Background Filler Designs

Cable Border

BORDERS AND CORNERS

An old wives' tale bids us quilt a continuous design in the border of a bridal quilt because a broken border foretells sorrow and strife. Continuous quilting designs magnify the framing effect of a border, but separate corner motifs are fine, too (unless you're superstitious).

How to mark the corner is an important decision when selecting a border design. Feathers, cables, and chains are wonderful, but they require planning to turn around the corners.

Whether you use a contrasting corner design or a connecting one, you should measure the repeat of the quilting design to be sure that it will fit neatly in the length of your border. For a continuous border corner, work out a motif that connects the vertical and horizontal borders appropriately. See *Log Cabin* (page 42) and *Star Path* (page 108) for examples. Many commercial stencils for border quilting designs include a corner.

HOUSEHOLD OBJECTS

We are surrounded by everyday objects that make wonderful quilting designs. Look around—here are some ideas to get you started.
• Cookie cutters are wonderful readymade templates for quilting designs— lined up like paper dolls or scattered across the quilt top.
• Circles are everywhere, in every size. Plates, bowls, cups and saucers, plastic containers, soup cans, coins, even mayonnaise jars can be used to trace circles.
• Hands and feet are always, well, at hand. Trace your own hands and feet or those of a child onto your quilt top—it tickles, but it's a cute quilting design. (*Editor's note:* Paws work well, too. I once dipped my cat's front paws in flour and "walked" her around a border so I could quilt authentic paw prints. She didn't enjoy it, but I did!)
• Leaves grow on trees. Pick one fresh, large leaf or several different kinds of leaves. Be sure to trace them before they dry out and crumble.

HAND QUILTING

For hand quilting, you will need quilting thread, which is heavier than sewing thread, and a thimble. Even if you're not used to a thimble, you'll find it a must for quilting to control the needle and to prevent it from digging into your fingertip. Quilting should be evenly spaced, with gaps between stitches about the same length as the stitches themselves. Uniformity is more important than the number of stitches per inch.

Put the layered quilt in a quilting hoop or frame. Position yourself so that the line of quilting angles from upper right to lower left, so you can quilt toward yourself. (Reverse directions if you are left-handed.)

Start with a size 7 or 8 "between," or quilting needle. (As your skill increases, try a smaller needle to make smaller stitches.) To keep the thread from snarling as you work, thread the needle with 18" of quilting thread *before* you cut the thread off the spool. Cut the thread and make a small knot in the clipped end.

Insert the needle through the quilt top, 1" from the point where the line of quilting will start. Slide the needle through the top and batting, without piercing the backing, and bring it up where the quilting will start. Pull the thread taut; then tug gently to pop the knot through the top into the batting.

1. Insert the needle straight down, about 1/16" from where the thread comes up. With your other hand under the quilt, feel for the needle point as it pierces the backing.

2. Push the fabric up from below as you rock the needle to a nearly horizontal position. Using the thumb of your sewing hand and the underneath hand, pinch a little hill in the fabric and push

the needle back through the quilt top. Rock the needle to an upright position to take another stitch—load three or four stitches on the needle before pulling it through, rocking and rolling to make each stitch.

Quilt until you have about 6" of thread left. Knot the thread close to the surface; then pop the knot through the top as before and clip the tail.

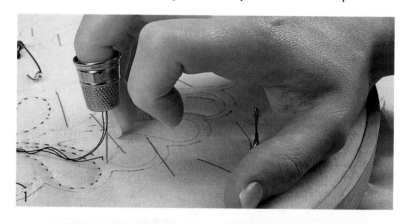

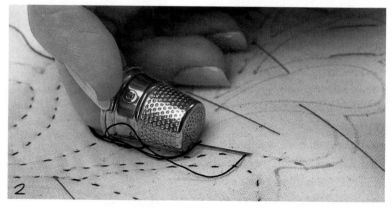

TYING

Pressed for time? Tying is the fastest and easiest way to secure the quilt layers. It's the best way to work with thick batting for puffy comforters. Tying is fine for polyester batting, but it may not be appropriate for cotton or silk battings, which require close quilting. Use pearl cotton, yarn, floss, or narrow ribbon for ties—anything that is stable enough to stay tightly tied. You'll need a sharp needle with an eye large enough to accommodate floss or yarn.

Thread the needle with about 7" of thread but do not knot the end. Starting in the center of your basted quilt top, take a small stitch through all three layers. Clip the thread, leaving a tail of thread about 3" long on each side of the stitch (Diagram A). Tie the two tails in a tight double knot (Diagram B). Make a tie at least every 6" across the surface of the quilt. Trim the tails of all the knots to the same length.

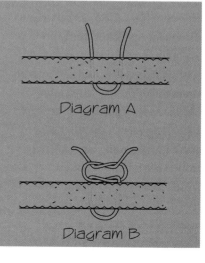

Diagram A

Diagram B

BACKGROUND FILLERS

Some quilts have background designs quilted in open spaces. Most fillers are patterns of lines stitched vertically, horizontally, or diagonally. Crossing lines make grids of squares or diamonds called cross-hatching. These fillers are easy to mark using only a marker and a ruler. *Kansas Troubles* (page 104) shows an effective use of background quilting. The grid of squares stitched in each large triangle complements the angles of the patchwork.

Not all background fillers are straight lines. Some filler patterns ignore the natural boundaries of the patchwork and create an allover design. Popular fillers of this type are clamshells, concentric circles, and half-circles.

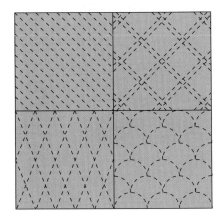

Background Filler Designs

Cable Border

BORDERS AND CORNERS

An old wives' tale bids us quilt a continuous design in the border of a bridal quilt because a broken border foretells sorrow and strife. Continuous quilting designs magnify the framing effect of a border, but separate corner motifs are fine, too (unless you're superstitious).

How to mark the corner is an important decision when selecting a border design. Feathers, cables, and chains are wonderful, but they require planning to turn around the corners.

Whether you use a contrasting corner design or a connecting one, you should measure the repeat of the quilting design to be sure that it will fit neatly in the length of your border. For a continuous border corner, work out a motif that connects the vertical and horizontal borders appropriately. See *Log Cabin* (page 42) and *Star Path* (page 108) for examples. Many commercial stencils for border quilting designs include a corner.

HOUSEHOLD OBJECTS

We are surrounded by everyday objects that make wonderful quilting designs. Look around—here are some ideas to get you started.

• Cookie cutters are wonderful ready-made templates for quilting designs—lined up like paper dolls or scattered across the quilt top.
• Circles are everywhere, in every size. Plates, bowls, cups and saucers, plastic containers, soup cans, coins, even mayonnaise jars can be used to trace circles.
• Hands and feet are always, well, at hand. Trace your own hands and feet or those of a child onto your quilt top—it tickles, but it's a cute quilting design. (*Editor's note:* Paws work well, too. I once dipped my cat's front paws in flour and "walked" her around a border so I could quilt authentic paw prints. She didn't enjoy it, but I did!)
• Leaves grow on trees. Pick one fresh, large leaf or several different kinds of leaves. Be sure to trace them before they dry out and crumble.

Getting Ready to Quilt

If you need to mark quilting designs, do it before the quilt is layered and basted. Free-style, outline, and in-the-ditch quilting do not require marking.

Marking

Before using any marker, test it on scraps of your fabric to be sure marks will wash out. The quilt top should be neatly pressed before marking.

1. The easiest way to mark a design is to use a stencil. Hundreds of quilting stencils are available at quilt shops and from mail-order sources.

2. To make your own stencil, trace a design onto freezer paper or peel-and-stick vinyl shelf paper; then use a craft knife to cut little slots along the lines of the design.

Backing

Each materials list specifies 45"-wide fabric needed for backing. Project instructions explain how to divide the fabric and construct the quilt back. As an alternative, yardage is given for wider fabric (54"–108" wide) for a seamless backing.

Backing doesn't have to be pieced from a single fabric. After all, if the top is scrappy, why not make the back scrappy, too? To save money and add a creative touch, some people piece scrappy backings from leftover fabric.

Batting

The batting you select should complement the nature and future use of your quilt. Batting is available in a variety of choices in fiber content, loft, ease of needling, softness, and washability.

Precut batting is available in five standard sizes. The batt listed for each project in this book is the most practical of the standard precut sizes. Some stores sell batting by the yard, and it may be more economical to purchase batting in that manner.

Cotton and *wool* battings give a quilt the flat, thin appearance of an antique quilt. The softness and thinness of these battings make it easier to quilt small, neat stitches. Be sure to read package labels for manufacturer's washing guidelines.

Bonded polyester batting is lightweight, easy to stitch, and washable. It has a slightly higher loft than cotton, which puts the quilting stitches in high relief. Bonded batting does not need a lot of quilting to keep it from shifting. Some brands give bonded batting a bad name because they are so stiff, so choose one that feels nice and soft.

Use thick batting for a puffy, comforter look. The thickness makes hand quilting difficult, so use thick batts for tied quilts.

No manufacturer has yet completely eliminated bearding, the migration of batting fibers through a quilt's outer layers of fabric. To minimize the visual effects of bearding, use black or gray batting for quilts made with predominantly dark fabrics.

Always read the information on the package before selecting a batting. When you take a batt from the package, remove wrinkles and fluff it out by spinning it in the dryer for a few minutes on an air-dry or cool setting.

Because of freight costs, some battings are distributed regionally instead of nationally. To get a batting that you particularly like, you may have to turn to a mail-order catalog. (See Mail-Order Resources, page 78.)

LAYERING

Choose a work surface where you can spread out the quilt—a large table, two tables pushed together, or a clean floor.

3. Fold the backing in half lengthwise and lightly crease it to create a center guideline. Fold the batting and quilt top in the same manner and mark center guidelines with pins.

Lay the backing right side down. Use masking tape to secure one long side of the backing to the work surface. On the opposite side, tug gently to remove wrinkles and folds; then tape that edge to the work surface. Repeat for the top and bottom edges. The back should be taut but not stretched out of shape.

Matching centers, place the batting on the backing. Smooth away wrinkles and be sure the batting is centered on the backing. Then center the quilt top on the batting, right side up. The batting and backing should be approximately 3" larger than the quilt top on all sides.

THREAD BASTING

4. Using white thread and a long hand-sewing needle, baste with a stitch 3"–4" long. (Some people like soft-sculpture needles or doll needles for basting.) Begin at the center of the quilt and work out to the edges in horizontal, vertical, and diagonal lines. If the quilt has sashing, baste along the sashing first. Before you start to quilt, check the back to be sure you haven't basted in puckers or pleats.

SAFETY-PIN BASTING

5. Rustproof safety pins are available in bulk at most quilt shops and fabric stores. For a full-size quilt, you will need approximately 500 (1"-long) pins.

Pin layers together, beginning at the center and working out to the edges in straight lines—horizontally, vertically, and diagonally. Position a pin about every 4". Work from the top only, pinning through all layers without reaching under the quilt. Check the back for puckers before you start to quilt.

HAND QUILTING

For hand quilting, you will need quilting thread, which is heavier than sewing thread, and a thimble. Even if you're not used to a thimble, you'll find it a must for quilting to control the needle and to prevent it from digging into your fingertip. Quilting should be evenly spaced, with gaps between stitches about the same length as the stitches themselves. Uniformity is more important than the number of stitches per inch.

Put the layered quilt in a quilting hoop or frame. Position yourself so that the line of quilting angles from upper right to lower left, so you can quilt toward yourself. (Reverse directions if you are left-handed.)

Start with a size 7 or 8 "between," or quilting needle. (As your skill increases, try a smaller needle to make smaller stitches.) To keep the thread from snarling as you work, thread the needle with 18" of quilting thread *before* you cut the thread off the spool. Cut the thread and make a small knot in the clipped end.

Insert the needle through the quilt top, 1" from the point where the line of quilting will start. Slide the needle through the top and batting, without piercing the backing, and bring it up where the quilting will start. Pull the thread taut; then tug gently to pop the knot through the top into the batting.

1. Insert the needle straight down, about ¹⁄₁₆" from where the thread comes up. With your other hand under the quilt, feel for the needle point as it pierces the backing.

2. Push the fabric up from below as you rock the needle to a nearly horizontal position. Using the thumb of your sewing hand and the underneath hand, pinch a little hill in the fabric and push

the needle back through the quilt top. Rock the needle to an upright position to take another stitch—load three or four stitches on the needle before pulling it through, rocking and rolling to make each stitch.

Quilt until you have about 6" of thread left. Knot the thread close to the surface; then pop the knot through the top as before and clip the tail.

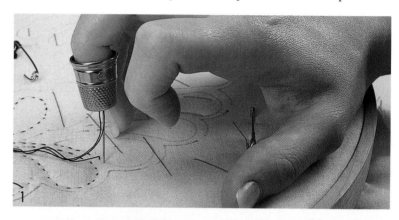

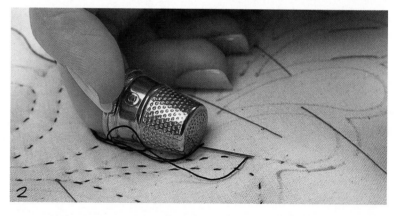

TYING

Pressed for time? Tying is the fastest and easiest way to secure the quilt layers. It's the best way to work with thick batting for puffy comforters. Tying is fine for polyester batting, but it may not be appropriate for cotton or silk battings, which require close quilting. Use pearl cotton, yarn, floss, or narrow ribbon for ties—anything that is stable enough to stay tightly tied. You'll need a sharp needle with an eye large enough to accommodate floss or yarn.

Thread the needle with about 7" of thread but do not knot the end. Starting in the center of your basted quilt top, take a small stitch through all three layers. Clip the thread, leaving a tail of thread about 3" long on each side of the stitch (Diagram A). Tie the two tails in a tight double knot (Diagram B). Make a tie at least every 6" across the surface of the quilt. Trim the tails of all the knots to the same length.

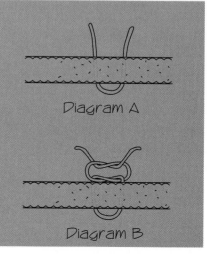

Diagram A

Diagram B

Machine Quilting

Choose continuous-line designs for machine quilting to minimize starts and stops. To machine-quilt straight lines, use an even-feed presser foot or walking foot. For free-motion quilting, use a darning foot.

For the top thread, use .004 monofilament "invisible" thread or regular sewing thread in a color that coordinates with the quilt. For the bobbin, use regular sewing thread that matches the backing.

Preparation

Roll the sides of the quilt to the middle and secure the rolls with bicycle clips. Or you may prefer to leave the quilt open and drape it over your shoulder as you work. If you're working on a large quilt, extend your work area by setting up tables to the left and behind the machine to help support the quilt while you work.

Set the machine's stitch length at 6–10 stitches per inch. Adjust the tension so that the bobbin thread does not pull to the top. Set the needle to stop in the down position or try to stop stitching with the needle down.

Turn the hand wheel to take a stitch, pulling the top thread to bring the bobbin thread to the surface. Hold onto both threads to prevent them from tangling when you begin quilting.

To secure the thread ends at the beginning and end of quilting lines, make tiny, close stitches for about ¼".

Quilting Straight Lines

1. Use your hands to assist the walking foot as you quilt. Spread the fabric slightly with your hands and gently push the quilt toward the foot to prevent puckering and reduce the drag on the fabric.

Free-Motion Quilting

Following a curved quilting design is a skill you must practice to master. Start with small projects that are easy to manipulate. Concentrate on following a design —smooth, even stitches will come with practice. Don't be discouraged if your first try is less than perfect.

Attach a darning foot or free-motion quilting foot; then lower the feed dogs or cover them. You don't need to adjust the stitch length; you will control the stitch length by manually moving the fabric.

2. Rest your fingertips on the fabric, with a hand on each side of the presser foot so you can move the fabric freely. To make even stitches, run the machine at a steady, medium speed and move the fabric smoothly and evenly so that the needle follows the design. Do not rotate the quilt; simply move the fabric forward, backward, and side to side.

BINDING

In this book, instructions are for double-fold binding. Double-layered binding is stronger than a single layer so it better protects the edges, where a quilt suffers the most wear and tear.

Cut 2"–2½" wide on either the bias or straight grain, the finished binding will be ⅜"–½" wide. Make wider binding when using thick batting.

Whether to make bias or straight-grain binding is a personal choice. With bias, woven threads crisscross over the quilt edge, creating a reinforced surface. With straight-grain, single threads run parallel to the edge, making the binding more likely to weaken with wear. Straight-grain binding is easier to make and often requires less fabric. If you make double-fold binding, straight-grain strips are usually satisfactory.

MAKING CONTINUOUS BIAS BINDING

1. Start with a fabric square. (Instructions state size of square needed.) Place pins at the middle of each side. Position pin heads toward the center at top and bottom edges. Point pin heads toward the outside edge at sides. Cut the square in half diagonally to get two triangles.

2. With right sides facing, match edges with pin heads pointed to the outside. Remove pins and join with a ¼" seam. Press the seam *open*.

3. On the wrong side of the fabric, mark cutting lines parallel to the long edges, spacing lines equal to the width of the binding strip. For a 2"-wide binding strip, draw lines 2" apart.

4. With right sides facing, match edges with pin heads pointed to the inside, offsetting one width of binding strip as shown. Join edges with a ¼" seam to make a tube. Press the seam open.

5. Begin cutting at the extended edge. Follow the drawn lines, rolling the tube around as you cut, until all fabric is cut in a continuous strip.

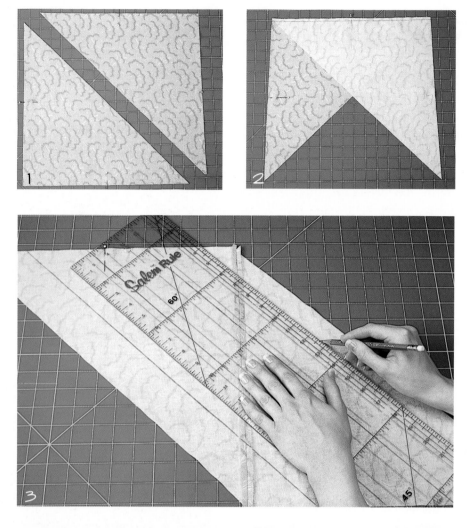

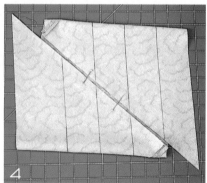

MAKING STRAIGHT-GRAIN BINDING

6. Cut the designated number of cross-grain strips. To join strips, lay them perpendicular to each other with right sides facing. Then stitch a diagonal seam across both strips. Trim seam allowances to ¼" and press them open. Make a continuous strip that is the length specified in the project instructions.

APPLYING BINDING

7. With wrong sides facing, fold the binding in half along the length of the strip and press.

8. Position the binding on the quilt's right side, in the middle of any side, aligning raw edges. Leave 3" of binding free before the point where you begin.

9. Stitch through all layers with a ¼" seam. Stop stitching ¼" from the quilt corner and backstitch. (Placing a pin at the ¼" point beforehand will show you where to stop.) Remove the quilt from the machine.

10. Rotate the quilt a quarter turn. Fold the binding straight up, away from the corner, and make a 45°-angle fold.

11. Bring the binding straight down in line with the next edge, leaving the top fold even with the raw edge of the previously sewn side. Begin stitching at the top edge, sewing through all layers. Stitch all corners in this manner.

12. Stop stitching as you approach the beginning point. Fold the 3" tail of binding over on itself and pin. The end of the binding will overlap this folded section. Continue stitching through all layers to 1" beyond the folded tail. Trim any extra binding.

13. Trim the batting and backing nearly even with the seam allowance, leaving a little extra to fill out the binding. Turn the binding over the seam allowance to the back. When turned, the beginning fold conceals the raw end of the binding.

14. Blindstitch the folded edge of the binding to the backing fabric. At back corners, fold the binding to miter it.

Quilters' Glossary

Acid-free. Tissue paper or boxes that are made without chemicals that can damage fabric over time. Available at art supply stores.

Appliqué. From the French word *appliquer,* meaning "to lay on." Used as a verb to refer to the process of sewing fabric pieces onto a background fabric. Used as a noun to refer to a piece of fabric that is sewn onto the background fabric.

Backing. The bottom layer of a finished quilt.

Batting. A soft filling between the patchwork top and the backing.

Bearding. Migration of loose batting fibers through the quilt top or backing.

Between. A short, small-eyed needle used for quilting. Available in several sizes, indicated by numbers; the higher the number, the shorter the needle.

Bias. The diagonal of a woven fabric, which runs at a 45° angle to the selvage. This is the direction that has the most stretch, making it ideal for curving appliqué shapes and for binding curved edges.

Bicycle clips. Metal or plastic bands designed to hold a cyclist's trousers close to the ankle while riding. Quilters use these clips to secure a rolled quilt during machine quilting.

Binding. A narrow strip of folded fabric that covers the raw edges of a quilt after it is quilted.

Bleeding. The run-off of dye when fabric is wet.

Chain piecing. Machine sewing in which units are sewn one after the other without lifting the presser foot or cutting the thread between units. Also called assembly-line piecing.

Charm quilt. A quilt composed of one shape in many fabrics (see *1000 Pyramids,* page 128). Traditionally, no two pieces are cut from the same fabric.

Cross-hatching. Lines of quilting that form a grid of squares or diamonds.

Diagonal corners. A quick-piecing technique that results in a contrasting triangle sewn to one or more corners of a square or rectangle. See page 17 for instructions. Also known as snowball corners.

Echo quilting. One or more lines of quilting that follow the outline of an appliqué piece, so the quilting repeats, or "echoes," the shape. A single line of echo quilting is called outline quilting.

Fat eighth. A 9" x 22" cut of fabric rather than a standard $\frac{1}{8}$ yard ($4\frac{1}{2}$" x 45").

Fat quarter. An 18" x 22" cut of fabric rather than a standard $\frac{1}{4}$ yard (9" x 45").

Four-patch. A block comprising four squares or units, joined in two rows of two squares each.

Fusible web. A material made of fibers that melt when heat is applied. Used to fuse two layers of fabric together.

In-the-ditch. Quilting stitches worked very close to or in the seam line.

Nine-patch. A block comprising nine squares or units, joined in three rows of three squares each.

Outline quilting. A single line of quilting that parallels a seam line, approximately $\frac{1}{4}$" away.

Pin matching. Using straight pins to align two seams so that they will meet precisely when a seam is stitched.

Prairie points. Triangles made from folded squares of fabric that are sewn into seams to provide a dimensional effect. Most often used as an edging.

Quick piecing. One of several techniques that eliminates some marking and cutting steps.

Quilt top. The upper layer of a quilt sandwich, it can be patchwork, appliquéd, or wholecloth. Quilting designs are marked and stitched on the top.

Quilting hoop. A portable wooden frame, round or oval, used to hold small portions of a quilt taut for quilting. A quilting hoop is deeper than an embroidery hoop to accommodate the thickness of the quilt layers.

Reversed patch. A patchwork piece that is a mirror image of another. To cut a reversed patch, turn the template over (reverse it).

Sashing. Strips of fabric sewn between blocks. Also known as lattice stripping.

Selvage. The finished edge of a woven fabric. More tightly woven than the rest of the fabric, selvage is not used for sewing because it may shrink differently when washed.

Set (Setting). The arrangement of joined blocks. See pages 148 and 149.

Sleeve. A fabric casing on the back of a quilt through which a dowel is inserted to hang the quilt on a wall. See instructions on page 23.

Straight grain. The horizontal and vertical threads of a woven fabric. Lengthwise grain runs parallel to the selvage. Cross-grain is perpendicular to the selvage.

String piecing. Randomly-sized scraps of fabric that are joined to make a base material, which is then cut into patchwork pieces. Sometimes worked on a foundation.

Strip piecing. A quick-piecing technique in which strips of different fabrics are joined and then cut into segments that become units of a patchwork block.

Template. A pattern guide, made of sturdy material, that is traced to mark the pattern shape onto fabric.

Triangle-square. A patchwork square that is composed of triangles. When two triangles are joined to make a square, these are called half-square triangles. When four triangles are joined to make a square, these are called quarter-square triangles. Triangles should be cut and sewn so that the straight grain falls on the square's outer edge.